P9-DHF-178

SCHAUMBURG TOWNSHIP DISTRICT LIBRARY

3 1257 01760 9529

WITHDRAWN

Schaumburg Township District Library
130 South Roselle Road
Schaumburg, Illinois 60193

THE
WORST
PERSON
IN THE
WORLD

Also by Keith Olbermann

The Big Show: A Tribute to ESPN's SportCenter
(co-authored by Dan Patrick)

WITHDRAWN

THE
WORST
PERSON
IN THE
WORLD

AND 202 STRONG
CONTENDERS

Keith Olbermann

SCHAUMBURG TOWNSHIP DISTRICT LIBRARY
130 SOUTH ROSELLE ROAD
SCHAUMBURG, ILLINOIS 60193

WILEY

John Wiley & Sons, Inc.

791.09
OLBERMANN, K

3 1257 01760 9529

Copyright © 2006 by Olbermann Broadcasting Empire, Inc. All rights reserved

Published by John Wiley & Sons, Inc., Hoboken, New Jersey
Published simultaneously in Canada

Design and composition by Navta Associates, Inc.

No part of this publication may be reproduced, stored in a retrieval system, or trans-mitted in any form or by any means, electronic, mechanical, photocopying, recording, scanning, or otherwise, except as permitted under Section 107 or 108 of the 1976 United States Copyright Act, without either the prior written permission of the Pub-lisher, or authorization through payment of the appropriate per-copy fee to the Copy-right Clearance Center, 222 Rosewood Drive, Danvers, MA 01923, (978) 750-8400, fax (978) 646-8600, or on the web at www.copyright.com. Requests to the Publisher for permission should be addressed to the Permissions Department, John Wiley & Sons, Inc., 111 River Street, Hoboken, NJ 07030, (201) 748-6011, fax (201) 748-6008, or online at http://www.wiley.com/go/permissions.

Limit of Liability/Disclaimer of Warranty: While the publisher and the author have used their best efforts in preparing this book, they make no representations or warranties with respect to the accuracy or completeness of the contents of this book and specifically dis-claim any implied warranties of merchantability or fitness for a particular purpose. No warranty may be created or extended by sales representatives or written sales materi-als. The advice and strategies contained herein may not be suitable for your situation. You should consult with a professional where appropriate. Neither the publisher nor the author shall be liable for any loss of profit or any other commercial damages, including but not limited to special, incidental, consequential, or other damages.

For general information about our other products and services, please contact our Customer Care Department within the United States at (800) 762-2974, outside the United States at (317) 572-3993 or fax (317) 572-4002.

Wiley also publishes its books in a variety of electronic formats. Some content that appears in print may not be available in electronic books. For more information about Wiley products, visit our web site at www.wiley.com.

Library of Congress Cataloging-in-Publication Data:

Olbermann, Keith, date.
  The worst person in the world: and 202 strong contenders / Keith Olbermann.
    p. cm.
  ISBN-13: 978-0-470-04495-7 (cloth)
  ISBN-10: 0-470-04495-0 (cloth)
  1. Celebrities—Conduct of life—Miscellanea. 2. Celebrities—United States—Conduct of life—Miscellanea. I. Title.
  CT105.O46 2007
  920.073—dc22

                                                                2006019133

Printed in the United States of America

10 9 8 7 6 5 4 3 2 1

They aren't really the *worst* persons in the world, of course.

Somewhere somebody's ending freedom, or sticking a shiv into a witness, or defrauding an orphan, or bombing a home. And there's almost nobody in this book who—in any kind of empirical analysis of *the* worst person in the world at a given moment—could truly hold a candle to any of them.

But my guys and gals have all, in their own ways, tried.

Orphans may have nothing to fear, and freedom is more likely to hurt itself laughing at them than to be hurt by their Rube Goldbergian machinations. But these *Worsts* (if you'll permit the term) are the mortal enemies of honesty and dignity, of selflessness and class.

In short—they'll do.

The epithet tracks directly to three of the great influences of my late childhood: George Carlin, Bob Elliott, and Ray Goulding. They were classified as comedians, yet each—Carlin in his remarkable solo career and Bob & Ray in their nonpareil tandem work—was a social commentator.

It was Carlin who startled me decades ago by the simple but irrefutable argument—the astonishing observation hidden inside the safety of a joke—that by the process of ranking, there truly had to be, somewhere, the worst doctor in the world. More terrifying still, he noted, "somebody has an appointment to see him *tomorrow!*"

Bob & Ray proclaimed themselves political neutrals (while allowing me a visit to their New York radio studios in 1974, Ray told me they didn't do political humor because "how could we top Watergate?"). Yet 20 years before, they had rung Joe McCarthy's neck every morning by mocking the Army-McCarthy hearings. Ray could do a perfect imitation of McCarthy's manic tone of "I'm just about to go crazy so better put some newspaper on the floor," and Bob captured the artificial self-deprecation of attorney Joseph Welch, giving him the priceless catchphrase "I'm just a simple showbiz lawyer."

They made McCarthy into a building commissioner in the fictional town of Skunkhaven, Long Island, and inserted him seamlessly into their unending and ad-libbed mock soap opera, "Mary Backstayge, Noble Wife." They utterly erased the politics of the equation and left only the absurdity. Morning after morning—when this was still dangerous stuff—their McCarthy and their Welch battled it out on one of New York's most-listened-to radio stations, over a plan to build a 30-story-tall private home.

When I heard them two decades later, "Mary Backstayge" was still running. The McCarthy and Welch vocal doppelgangers were long gone, but in their place was an ominous character, the W.P.I.T.W.—the Worst Person in the World—who made no comments, but was limited to a series of crunching and slurping sound effects. He invariably turned up while the other characters were dining. "Look at him," Ray would say in the gummy voice of Calvin Hoogevin. "He's eating the sandwich right through the wax paper." Soon after the W.P.I.T.W.'s appearance, his true identity was revealed, on the air. He was John Simon, the venerable reviewer of *New York* magazine—who had given Bob & Ray's Broadway show the only bad review it ever got.

So there are the primogenitors of my "Worst" lists—complete with Carlin's touch of amazed terror, the Bob & Ray conviction that no weapon succeeds like satire, and that little extra soupçon of revenge, personal and egotistical, and somehow cleansed of both characteristics by the stark admission that it *is* revenge.

For many months, I had contemplated introducing a segment to my nightly MSNBC newscast, *Countdown*, that somehow combined all these elements with which I was inculcated as a boy. I had tentatively thought of "The S List"—but that seemed way too generic. And then one day late in June 2005, two things happened within hours of each other. First, I heard a tape of one of those Bob

& Ray soap operas with the W.P.I.T.W. eating not just the wax paper but also the brown bag in which his lunch sat. Then, I read Alessandra Stanley's review in the *New York Times* suggesting that our network needed to cancel Tucker Carlson's new show. This rang as the quintessence of unfairness. MSNBC had been blasted, for years, for never giving new programs any time to develop. Tucker had been on the air less than two weeks.

Suddenly the two names merged. "Worst Person in the World . . . Alessandra Stanley." We premiered the segment that night, and setting the standards for a certain kind of fairness, Stanley proved only a runner-up. I have never placed my prejudice ahead of somebody else's superior mendaciousness. Here is that first segment:

> A new feature debuting tonight: *Countdown's* list of today's top three nominees for "The Worst Person in the World."
>
> Number three: Alessandra Stanley, TV writer or critic or something—it's hard to tell what—of the *New York Times*. As her latest article suggests, if she keeps passing off that many dubious opinions as anonymous facts, she may soon lose her . . . situation.
>
> Number two: Saddam Hussein. This is separate from the whole dictator thing. He has now threatened to sue the newspaper that first ran the photo of him in his underwear. As its headline today ran: "You and what army?"
>
> And number one: Robert Novak.
>
> We *still* know what you did last summer! Well, summer *before* last summer.
>
> The Worst Person in the World.

And from there we were rolling, devoting about 90 seconds of each news hour to this odd little list.

The mighty and the anonymous alike have made the nightly "The Worst Persons in the World" trifecta—from Robert Novak to Scott Peterson to the Ronald McDonald who held up a Wendy's. And there have really been only a handful of complaints.

The foremost of them came from John Gibson and Bill O'Reilly of Fox News. Evidently they don't like being considered among the Worst Persons in the World—even though they clearly *are*.

O'Reilly first, because he was funnier.

Late in December 2005, Ted Baxter's evil twin did some sort of year-end wrap-up of his rants and distortions. It was a self-loofah'ing of congratulation, for the nightly disaster his program means for the truth. "Speaking of disasters, our competitor at MSNBC is a notorious smear merchant. So far this month, December, *The Factor*'s third rerun at 4:00 in the morning has beaten the MSNBC's original 8:00 program more than 50 percent of the time. Unbelievable."

A couple of things to note here: We never *claimed* O'Reilly's program doesn't draw vastly more viewers than does ours. The years 2005 and 2006 saw his ratings slide and ours grow by about 50 percent, but the gap is still pronounced, and, after all, some time in the 1970s or 1980s we stopped worrying about the quality of things, and were concerned only about how many of them were *sold*.

To borrow a phrase—hey, 800 billion flies can't be wrong.

But it is curious, isn't it, that O'Reilly branded me a "smear merchant" and yet instead of trying to refute even *one* of the hateful things we've quoted him as saying or doing, he instead turned to the ratings. That's probably because the only things we've "smeared" O'Reilly with were his own quotes.

To borrow another phrase—when you're as guilty as he is, change the subject.

Unfortunately I now have to change the subject to John Gibson, and this remains greatly painful because I really don't know why he decided to try to destroy himself, but he did. O'Reilly, after all, is one of those *blissful* idiots who can rationalize anything. That doing that long *enough* usually results in a complete collapse is well known, and his clock is clearly ticking in that regard.

But even *he* was not so functionally stupid as to deny saying things that were preserved on tape—which is what poor John Gibson did.

John had originally made the Worst Person list, thusly:

> But the winner, and this one comes with great personal pain because we were friends when he worked here and thereafter, John Gibson.
>
> Selling his new book about this phony baloney war on Christmas, John revealed a very ugly side to himself. He is one

4

of those people who think all religions but his are mistaken. You know, the way a lot of these religious nut bag terrorists think. "I would think," Gibby said on a syndicated radio show, "if somebody is going to be—have to answer for following the wrong religion, they are not going to have to answer to me. We know who they're going to have to answer to."

I'd tell you which religion John thinks is the only one that's right, but what's the difference? It's not the faith that's the issue. It's the intolerance. John Gibson, today's Worst Person in the World.

John first complained about that on his radio program, then he called all manner of people at NBC and MSNBC, and then he went to town on his television show: "I find myself being misquoted or the quotes taken out of context in order to build outrage against me. . . . [I'm called] "names like 'fathead' and the 'worst something or other' for things I really did not say . . .

"Friday one of my former colleagues repeated a misquote to justify saying some truly disgusting things about me. Condescendingly, he 'tisk tisked' that he used to like me. I frankly doubt it. Otherwise, why be so willing to believe trash?"

Well, John, I *believed* it because it was true—and it was on *tape*. I'm afraid he was, at best, suffering from amnesia. At worst, he was just flat-out pretending something never happened.

John Gibson's remarks about religions being wrong and those who believe them having to answer for them came on a show hosted by a Janet Parshall, broadcast by Salem Radio Networks, on November 17, 2005—and they're on tape. The Web site Media Matters for America has a transcript and an audio link, and I'm afraid there's no ambiguity whatsoever.

This is what he said, without edit or interruption of context:

John Gibson: "The whole point of this is that the tradition, the religious tradition of this country is tolerance, and that the same sense of tolerance that's been granted by the majority to the minority over the years ought to go the other way too. Minorities ought to have the same sense of tolerance about the majority religion—Christianity—that they've been granted about their religions over the years."

Janet Parshall: "Exactly. John, I have to tell you, let me linger for a minute on that word 'tolerance.' Because first of all, the people who like to promulgate that concept are the worst violators. They cannot tolerate Christianity, as an example."

John Gibson: "Absolutely. I know—I know that."

Janet Parshall: "And number two, I have to tell you, I don't know when they held this election and decided that tolerance was a transcendent value. I serve a god who, with a finger of fire, wrote, he will have no other gods before him. And he doesn't tolerate sin, which is why he sent his son to the cross, but all of a sudden now, we jump up and down and celebrate the idea of tolerance. I think tolerance means accommodation, but it doesn't necessarily mean acquiescence or whole-hearted acceptance."

John Gibson: "No, no, no. If you figure that—listen, we get a little theological here, and it's probably a bit over my head, but I would think if somebody is going to be—have to answer for following the wrong religion, they're not going to have to answer to me. We know who they're going to have to answer to."

Janet Parshall: "Right."

John Gibson: "And that's fine. Let 'em. But in the meantime, as long as they're civil and behave, we tolerate the presence of other religions around us without causing trouble, and I think most Americans are fine with that tradition."

Sigh.

There is always the possibility—however remote—that it wasn't John Gibson speaking, but merely some kind of professional John Gibson Impersonator, or a vocal impressionist as gifted as Ray Goulding doing his Joe McCarthy in 1954. In which case, the *impersonator* is clearly the Worst Person not just of the night, but of all time.

Otherwise, that's really the whole shebang right there.

That phrase "wrong religion" actually reads worse in context, doesn't it? It's the same kind of misunderstanding and perversion of faith to which we react in horror when we see it in terrorists who have twisted religions for their own purposes. Might as well have been commentators on some All-Access Al Qaeda show on Al Jazeera talking about infidels.

And by the way, don't you get this creepy feeling of embarrassment when somebody trying desperately to be holier-than-thou promptly *mis*quotes the bible? "I serve a god who, with a finger of fire," you just read the transcript of Janet Parshall saying, "wrote, he will have no other gods before him."

Actually, Ms. Parshall, as any of us who've actually *read* the bible know, the first commandment is *"Thou* shalt have no other gods before me."* That's not just a difference in pronouns—he's demanding exclusivity from those who believe in him. Nothing in there saying *other* people can't serve *other* gods in which they believe.

I've strayed from the main topic, probably because it is awfully painful. Whether he thinks me insincere or not, I really did like Gibby: hardworking, always there to cover a shift or help out in any way he could. Instead, he devolved into denying he said some truly despicable things—things recorded for posterity—and worse, he tried to blame those hateful things on me. Ordinarily when somebody gets caught saying something as intolerant as this, their choices are (a) to apologize, (b) to resign, or (c) to make sure there's no tape and try to lie their way out of it.

John chose "d"—blame it on somebody else.

The audio clip was the definitive answer (we sometimes spend hours looking for verification of "Worst" tips, and postpone nominations for days, because unlike other newscasters and commentators, I have this silly idea in my head that the whole point of any criticism is that it has to be based on discernible *facts*). I said on *Countdown* that I hoped John would have the self-respect to acknowledge what he said and to leave the airways for good, because, between the remark and the denial, he had—sadly—forfeited his right to stay here.

He didn't. But neither did he bring the matter up again on the air. Or phone again, as he did some of our twentieth-century colleagues at MSNBC and NBC News. Or say much of anything else that anybody cared about.

Of Mr. O'Reilly, you probably know. As his appearances on the list increased in number and frequency (hell, one night he won all three places), he began to criticize me indirectly, calling out my bosses on the air—but never me, not by name—and eventually jumping the proverbial shark by announcing an online petition to get me fired (all of us on *Countdown* signed, me included) and then infamously threatening a caller to his radio call-in show with visits from "local authorities" and "Fox Security" because the caller had had the audacity to mention *my* name on *Mr. O'Reilly's* air.

Exit Mr. O'Reilly's grasp of reality, stage left.

Before we get to some of the individual nightly lists, I must say that the "Worsts" have achieved a kind of unexpected status as electronic red badges of courage in the cultural battles. A conservative colleague of Gibson and O'Reilly, whose name I must not divulge because his good-natured willingness to take criticism and spoofing would make him suspect in the eyes of his less brainy brethren, recently buttonholed me and *complained* that he hadn't been one of the Worst Persons. "It's my goal in life," he said with a laugh. I told him he simply had yet to say or do something totally indefensible.

He laughed again. "I'll just have to keep trying."

He may or may not. But this much is undoubtedly true: Dozens of others certainly *will*.

Our panel holds
a grudge.

Alone in This Universe

The bronze goes to New York State assemblyman Willis Stevens. He was monitoring one of those online discussion groups, 300 of his constituents in the city of Brewster, when he decided to send an e-mail to one of his assistants. He hit the wrong button. Instead, he sent it to all 300 people in the group. The e-mail read, "Just watching the idiots pontificate."

The silver: A holdover from yesterday. Robert Novak, still one of the worst people in the world.

And the winner . . .

Tom Cruise! And this has got nothing to do with Brooke Shields or psychiatry or the movie *War of the Worlds*. He has another controversy running. Asked by the German tabloid *Bildt* if he believes in aliens, Cruise snapped at this guy, too. "Yes, of course. Are you really so arrogant as to believe we are alone in this universe?"

Maybe Tom is from another planet.

Tom Cruise, *today's Worst Person in the World!*

Chest for Hire

At the bronze level: Whoever runs the campus police at Texas State University in San Marcos. A man named Dave Newman saw a stranger drowning in the swirling San Marcos River. Newman went in and saved him. As he got out of the river, Newman was handcuffed by a Texas State University cop, who said Newman had ignored repeated warnings to get out of the river.

The silver goes to French president Jacques Chirac. He thought he was just passing time with Germany's Gerhard Schroeder and Vladimir Putin of Russia. He didn't know there were three translators and a reporter present as he started an international food fight about the English. "The only thing they have ever given European farming is Mad Cow [disease]. You can't trust people who cook as badly as that. After Finland, it's the country with the worst food."

But today's winner . . .

Paula Jones, not only for complaining to the *New York Daily News* that she's been left out of the Bill Clinton Presidential Library, but for threatening to visit the library. If some company pays her to do so, she'd wear its logo on her T-shirt.

Paula Jones, *today's Worst Person in the World!*

Free the Press

The bronze: Members of the band Razor Light. They appeared in the Live 8 worldwide charity concerts over the weekend. Pink Floyd donated its profits from additional album sales to the charity. Annie Lennox did, as did the the Who. Razor Light says it's keeping all the money it will make off the gig.

Ladies and gentlemen, this was Razor Light's farewell appearance. Good-bye, everybody.

The silver: O.J. Simpson. Police were summoned to his home in Kendall, Florida, when his girlfriend attacked Simpson and Simpson's friend, who then said she went after O.J. like a vampire and he just stood there and took it. Simpson did nothing wrong, so why has he been nominated?

Because our panel holds a grudge.

But your winner . . .

Judge Thomas Hogan of the U.S. district court in Washington. He sent a reporter to jail. The reporter might be wrong. She might be right. The law might be wrong. It might be right. But any way you cut it, you, sir, sent an American reporter to an American jail two days after the 229th anniversary of the Declaration of Independence.

Judge Thomas Hogan, *today's Worst Person in the World!*

Time to Buy

JULY 8, 2005

The bronze goes to Drew Sanders, a community center teen boys' basketball coach in Staten Island, New York, who allegedly has an unusual way of teaching at least one of his players how to shoot. When he missed, police say, Sanders would throw the 15-year-old boy over his knees and then spank him with a paddle.

And the silver: A number of London hotels reported by the BBC and other news organizations there to have raised room rates the night after the subway bombing, one man saying he was charged $435 for what is usually an $80 room.

But the winner . . .

Our old friend, Brit Hume of Fox, who actually said on the air at 1:25 yesterday afternoon, after the bombings in London, "My first thought when I heard, just on a personal basis—when I heard there had been this attack, and I saw the futures this morning, which were really in the tank,"—he's referring to the futures options on the stock market—"I thought, Hmm, time to buy."

Brit Hume, *a great humanitarian and today's*
Worst Person in the World!

The Lion Is Meat

At the bronze level, there's baseball's top camera basher, Kenny Rogers. Today he turned himself in to the cops on the assault charges one of the cameramen brought, and gets a mug shot soon to be appearing on his bubble-gum card.

The silver: Wayne La Pierre, president of the ever-popular NRA, the National Rifle Association. He's moving the group's 2007 convention out of Columbus, Ohio, after the city council there passed a ban on assault weapons. As a result, La Pierre tells the city, 65,000 people will not be coming to your wonderful convention center. Hundreds of exhibitors will not fill your halls with their latest guns, outdoor gear, and hunting accessories.
I'm confused. Oh, I get it. He thinks that's a punishment! OK.

But today's winner . . .

Debra Lafave, the 24-year-old Tampa schoolteacher accused of having had sex with a 14-year-old student. Her attorney says plea negotiations have broken off because the prosecution demanded Lafave go to the Florida state women's penitentiary, and, quoting him, "To place an attractive young woman in that kind of hellhole is like putting a piece of raw meat in with the lions."
Raw meat in with the lions. I guess that's how you could have described putting those 14-year-old boys in her classroom, huh? Huh?

Debra Lafave, *today's Worst Person in the World!*

Try Being Sorry

At the bronze level, there's Steven Segal. He is releasing an album on which he sings everything from blues to Jamaican dance-hall music. There is a kernel of good news: maybe he won't seem like such a lousy actor.

At the silver level, Gary Moody, the Maine man arrested for being a peeping tom while under the seat of a ladies' outhouse. His excuse while pleading not guilty? He was in the toilet tank looking for his wedding ring. That's the best he can do?

But the winner is . . .

Baseball pitcher Kenny Rogers. Long after his supposedly heart-felt public apologies, he turned himself in to police on charges of assaulting two TV cameramen. Another cameraman filmed him getting booked, and Rogers yelled at him: "You must be pretty proud of yourself."

When the cameraman said he was just doing his job, Rogers replied: "Yeah—your job. That's just your excuse." Kenny, a quick helpful hint: next time you say you're sorry, try being sorry.

Once again . . .

*Baseball's **Kenny Rogers**, today's*
Worst Person in the World!

16

Deferred Success

At the bronze level, we've got James Mazzarelli, who owns a small zoo in Litchfield, Connecticut. He says six customers tried to leave the place without paying. Police say he responded by locking them in the zoo with the animals.

Then there's Publicist X, the anonymous spokesperson for Fox News who today continued to issue personal attacks on the reporters and executives of the actual cable news networks. We don't know who X is. However, Fox News's vice president of media relations is named Irena Briganti, and X presumably works for her. Ms. Briganti certainly doesn't want to appear as covering up for a cowardly, insecure, ashamed, gutless employee, so she should fire him or her posthaste.

But the winner . . .

Liz Beattie, a retired primary school teacher in England, who is leading the teachers' union there in trying to change the education system so that no student will ever fail again. A student would be able to bank the correct parts of a failed test. He wouldn't get an F.

He'd get a "Deferred Success"!

***Liz Beattie**, today's Worst Person in the World!*

Deceased, Do Not Contact

First, there's Dianne Applegate, director of the Fountain County, Indiana, 4H council pageant, which annually selects a local teenage girl as queen. This year, judges gave Jordan Snoddy more votes, but the pageant declared Sarah Rice the queen. Why? Sarah Rice is the niece of Dianne Applegate, director of the Fountain County, Indiana, 4H council pageant.

The silver: The people behind a water-gun tournament in New York City. Unfortunately, right at this point in our fearful lives, they're calling the thing "Street Wars" and telling would-be participants, "The killing begins August 1. Street Wars is an assassination tournament. You can hunt your target down any way you see fit. Then you win, but first, live in fear." Nice timing.

But the winner . . .

Pat Kachura, a senior vice president of ethics at the Direct Marketing Association. Recognizing the pain that could be caused when a telemarketer calls up and asks to talk to Joe Smith, only to hear from his wife that Joe Smith died last month, the Direct Marketing Association says that out of its sensitivity, it will establish a new "Deceased, do not contact" list.

And you only have to pay the telemarketers a dollar to sign your dead loved one up.

Pat Kachura, *today's Worst Person in the World!*

Me Included

Kind of a grim theme here.

The bronze to one of the permanent residents, Bill O'Reilly, caught lying on air again. He told his audience that our sister network, CNBC, would not provide him with a statement about an interview Donny Deutsch conducted on the air there, but CNBC had already issued the statement. O'Reilly just didn't like it, so he pretended it didn't happen.

You know, just like the rest of the stuff on his show.

Then there's Ken Livingstone, the mayor of London. You know, it is one thing when plainclothes police chase and kill an innocent man on his way to work because they think he's a suicide bomber. But did Livingstone really have to say, "This tragedy has added another victim to the toll of deaths for which the terrorists bear responsibility"?

You don't think the cops bear some of the responsibility, pal?

But the winner . . .

The news media for this same event. And I am putting my picture up there because I did this, too. When the police in London said Friday that they'd killed that poor man because he had strong connections to the failed bomb attempts on Thursday, we all just assumed that they knew what they were doing. They didn't. And neither did we. We all just bought their story.

Well, that won't happen again. Not here.

The media, me included, *today's Worst Persons in the World!*

She's Really Crazy

JULY 28, 2005

First, the bronze goes to the people at Massport, the highway authority in Massachusetts. They replaced six suicide prevention hotline signs that had been mysteriously moved earlier this month from a Boston bridge. One problem: the new signs for the suicide hotline have the wrong phone number.

The silver: The Reverend Jim Grove of York, Pennsylvania. Everybody is entitled to an opinion about abortion, but Reverend Grove's opinion may lead to the cancellation of York's traditional Halloween parade. The city says it cannot run the legal risk of authorizing Grove's anti-abortion Halloween float. The title should be enough to explain why. It is called Dr. Butcher's Chop Shop of Choice Cuts.

But the winner?

That would be Channoah Green. Police say she got mad at her 4-year-old son because he would not sit down in the car, so she pulled over and made him get out—on the side of the highway near Falls Church, Virginia, at ten o'clock at night. When he tried to get back into the car, she drove off, hitting him with the car and driving 90 miles away.

The boy is OK, just scrapes. A neighbor says of the "mother," "That's out of character. She's really crazy about the boy."

Well, neighbor, sounds like you're half right.

Channoah Green, *today's Worst Person in the World!*

Designated Passenger

The bronze winner: The umpire in the Massachusetts state Little League tournament game. When a coach from the Methuen team shouted instructions in Spanish, the umpire stopped the game and ordered all players to speak English only. Supervisors have apologized.

Note, please, the umpire is unnamed. It's a bad sign when the name of the umpire in a ballgame is a secret.

Also nominated, the folks on the Web site Betonsports. Today they made it possible for to you bet on whether or not the appointment of John Roberts in the Supreme Court will mean *Roe v. Wade* will be overturned.

But the winner?

Trevon Smith of Fontana, California. Somebody stole his car. He wanted it back. He didn't want to wait, so he told police that his 4-year-old niece was in the car. She wasn't. He's been arrested.

Trevon Smith, *today's Worst Person in the World!*

This is from somebody who ran away in terror from a pie.

Let's Play Two

The bronze nominee: An unnamed man from Macedonia who drove into the gas station at Pesaro, Italy, with his wife and daughter, so they could use the restroom. Six hours later, six hours, he says, he noticed she was not in the backseat with the kid. He had driven off without his wife.

Also, there's Joe Lucero of Salt Lake City. Police allege he tried unsuccessfully to rob two women, then tried unsuccessfully to break into an apartment, then tried unsuccessfully to drive a jeep he had carjacked and rolled the thing, then tried unsuccessfully to break into some more apartments, then kicked in a door, tried unsuccessfully to get a woman to give him her baby, then tried unsuccessfully to flee by jumping out the window, all in about ten minutes.

But the winner . . .

Baseball pitcher Kenny Rogers, the guy who assaulted two TV news photographers and was suspended for 20 games. First, he apologized, supposedly sincerely. Then, at his arraignment, he yelled at another TV photographer. And today, he got his suspension reduced to 13 games, so he can play again tomorrow.

***Kenny Rogers**, today's Worst Person in the World!*

Cleaning Up Our Streets

AUGUST 10, 2005

The bronze-level nominee: David Teel from Grasse in southern France. He's 81, so they gave him a suspended sentence of a year in jail. Last month, he was awakened from his nap by noisy helicopters. So, he shot at them with a hunting rifle. They were there trying to put out a nearby forest fire.

Also nominated, James C. Garrett, insisting he deserves a spot on the ballot in the race for mayor of Seattle, even though he was convicted four years ago of felony assault on the then mayor of Seattle. He said he should be excused for that because he is suffering from what he called post-traumatic slavery syndrome.

But the winner . . .

Officer Dan Bray of the police department of Hooksett, New Hampshire. He went to the home of Natasha Fryou and handed out a citation for littering in the amount of $288, Officer Dan claiming he saw Natasha throw at least three objects out of her car window the other day and she has to pay up. Natasha's parent spoke on her behalf, saying she did throw or drop a small ball out the window.

The alleged perpetrator, Natasha, is 4 years old.

Officer Dan Bray, *today's Worst Person in the World!*

Joy Ride

AUGUST 10, 2005

Legendary and tragic was the story of the New York Mets baseball fan who decided to ride one of those big movable trash dumpsters down the ramps at Shea Stadium 25 years ago. He forgot that the ramp made turns and that those dumpsters could not.

He has now been matched by a fan of the rival New York Yankees, who decided to test the strength of the protective screen behind home plate at Yankee Stadium in much the way you might test to see if your hair would actually burn if you lit your head on fire.

Scott Harper jumped down onto the screen from the upper deck. The game telecast did not capture his 40-foot leap visually, but a camera mounted under the screen there registered the impact as Harper, 18 years old, from the New York City suburb of Armonk, finished what he told three friends he was going to do—see if the net would really support his weight.

It did. Harper then learned that the police could also support his weight. They carted him off on a stretcher, his head later immobilized in a neck brace. He was not seriously injured, not even by the police, the easiest observation being that of course he wasn't injured; he had fallen on his least vital organ, his brain.

Harper has now just been charged with trespassing upon the playing area of a professional sporting event. Also reckless endangerment, criminal mischief, and other unnamed violations. He was arraigned late this afternoon at the Bronx Criminal Courthouse, which is a big building you can almost see over the right center field fence at Yankee Stadium. He has been released, apparently on his own recognizance, and he faces up to a year in jail.

Incredibly, this has happened before in several other ballparks, where players have fallen or fans have fallen out of upper decks, intentionally or otherwise. It happened at Yankee Stadium five years ago. A 24-year-old guy fell out and landed on the screen and was knocked out. Nobody was really ever sure if that was deliberate or not.

And it's worth mentioning that the backstop tore when he hit it. He could have gone right through and landed on somebody else, which is maybe the not-so-fun part of this.

No reason to stop selling beer at ballgames. Naah.

***Scott Harper**, an Honorary Worst Person in the World!*

What Would Be the E-ticket Ride?

AUGUST 11, 2005

First there's Jason Brahim of Murrysville, Pennsylvania. He is charged with disorderly conduct after police claim he got angry on the golf course and beat a goose to death with his club. And he lied about how many strokes it took him.

The silver nominee: Professor Mark Bellis of John Moores University in Liverpool in England. He is one of the researchers behind the new study that could scare the Shinola out of you if you're a parent of either gender. It suggests one out of every 25 fathers in the world is raising another's man child, unknowingly. Professor Bellis has also deduced that the principal cause of this might just be marital infidelity.
You think?

But the winner . . .

Counselor Lam Kitzin of Hong Kong, noting that in the last eight years, 20 people have killed themselves in one hotel on Cheung Chau Island there. He suggested that when Hong Kong's new Disneyland opens in September, Cheung Chau Island should convert that island into a suicide-themed amusement park. He did not say which one you were supposed to go to first.

Counselor Lam Kitzin, *today's Worst Person in the World!*

When Fishes Don't Behave

AUGUST 12, 2005

The bronze level: We're not sure which side is guilty here, the employees or the company, but whichever, they get nominated. The other doesn't. The Equal Employment Opportunity Commission has sued Tyson Foods. Two employees say that at the Tyson plant, in Ashland, Alabama, somebody put up a sign over a bathroom reading "Whites only."

The silver goes to Charles Dryling, Jr. He had a pipe bomb in his bag as he tried to board a flight from Oklahoma City to Atlanta. He explained to the authorities that he had built it for fun and forgotten he had left it in his bag.

But the winner . . .

The folks at the Florida Aquarium in Tampa. This is like that scene in Monty Python's *The Meaning of Life* when the guy goes into the restaurant, and there's a big fish tank and all the fish are talking about the fish who is on the plate. At a food fundraiser at the aquarium there, seven chefs set up among the tanks and pools in a sushi showdown. They're serving sushi at the aquarium.

Flipper! Charlie, when fishes don't behave, this is what fishes get!

The folks at the Florida Aquarium in Tampa,
today's Worst Persons in the World!

Glove Cleaner

AUGUST 16, 2005

Nominated at the bronze level right here on MSNBC today: David Horowitz, author of *Unholy Alliance: Radical Islam and the American Left*. Having written a book with that kind of happy title, he actually said of Cindy Sheehan this afternoon, "This is a hateful woman with a hateful message."

Like her politics or hate them, this is a gold-star mother, sir. Shut your mouth.

Instead of the silver, we have, for the first time ever, a tie for the winner.

First, pitcher Livan Hernandez of baseball's Washington Nationals. Upset at being removed from a game, he fired his glove into the stands at RFK Stadium in Washington and then was upset when the fan who grabbed it would not give it back.

However, the fan is no day at the beach either. He offered to give it back in exchange for playoff tickets this year, season tickets next year, and $18,000 in cash.

Livan Hernandez and the fan who has all of his glove,
today's Worst Persons in the World!

Rush to Judgment

AUGUST 17, 2005

Nominated at the bronze level: In coastal Scotland, police report that some people while away the late summer afternoons by going to the cliffs and throwing rocks at the people who live and drive below. A policeman warned them, "Playing near cliffs is dangerous, boys." Why did you tell them, sir?

Also, the fine folks at Austin Community College in Texas. Carl Basham said he was denied the state residence discount for tuition. He has to pay $2,600 a semester instead of $500 because they say he spent too much time living out of state. Well it's true, Carl has been away, serving, he says, two tours in Iraq.

But the winner . . .

The irrepressible Rush Limbaugh. On the radio, he said, "Cindy Sheehan is just Bill Burkett. Her story is nothing more than forged documents. There's nothing about it that's real." I guess she made up that dead son in Iraq business!

He also referred to her supporters as dope-smoking FM types. I guess the painkillers wipe out your memory along with your ethics.

Rush Limbaugh, *today's Worst Person in the World!*

A Golden Predicament

AUGUST 17, 2005

There is nothing wrong with an unpopular opinion.

Nor is there anything wrong with a subversive one, or a crazy one. This country was founded on opinions that were deemed by the powers-that-were to be unpopular, subversive, and crazy. Dissent—even when that dissent strays from logic or humanity–is our lifeblood. But if you have one of those opinions, and you express it in public, honesty and self-respect require you to own up to it.

Unless you're Rush Limbaugh.

On his daily radio soap opera, on August 15, Limbaugh said, "Cindy Sheehan is just Bill Burkett. Her story is nothing more than forged documents, there's nothing about it that's real. . . ." The complete transcript of the 860 words that surround those quotes can be found at the bottom of this entry.

Yet, apparently there was something so unpopular, so subversive, and so crazy about those remarks that he has found it necessary to deny he said them—even when there are recordings and transcripts of them—and to brand those who've claimed he said them as crackpots and distorters. More over, that amazing temple to himself, his Web site, has been scrubbed clean of all evidence of these particular remarks, and to "prove" his claim that he never made the remarks in question on August 15, he has misdirected visitors to that site to transcripts and recordings of remarks he made on August 12.

Limbaugh is terrified. And he has reason to be.

Understand this about Limbaugh. He doesn't believe half the junk he spouts. I've met him, and had pleasant enough conversations with him, twice—at the 1980 World Series, when he was still a mid-level baseball flunky with a funny name, and once in the mid-'90s at ESPN, when he was just beginning his campaign to get a toehold there. He is a quiet, almost colorless man who, if he could be guaranteed similar success in sportscasting, would sell out the sheep who follow his every word—and would do it before close of business today.

But with that ESPN bid having gone up in flames just under two years ago, and sports forever closed off to him, he's gotten into what the novelist Robert Graves called a "Golden Predicament"— overwhelming success in a field he really had no intention of pursuing—and he has to keep churning this stuff out every day. And when you're just free-associating to kill time and keep the dittoheads happy, you sometimes drive right off the end of the pier.

Like on August 15.

Since we declared Limbaugh "the Worst Person in the World" two nights later for the remarks about Sheehan, he has had the transcript of his pier-dive expunged (even though he initially thought so much of it that it was posted as a "featured quote" for paying subscribers to his Web site). Simultaneously, the hapless Brent Bozell, who runs that scam called the Media Research Center, declared that I was guilty of "distortion" in quoting the Sheehan remarks.

Well, as you'll see below, the only distortion here is that which lingers in Limbaugh's ears. His remarks about Sheehan were so strongly embraced by at least one of his fans that they were preserved on another Web site, and we can present them in full here. You will notice that nothing has been taken out of context, nothing in the minutes before or the minutes afterward mitigates the utter callousness and infamy of his comments about Sheehan.

A reminder that that's Cindy Sheehan, Gold-Star Mother, who when I asked her bluntly if President Bush wasn't serving her purposes more by not seeing her, was honest enough to answer "Yes" without hesitation. And it's Rush Limbaugh, who so believes in his case against her that he's too afraid to admit he said this (and who, by the way, has since said of her that "I'm weary of even having to express sympathy . . . we all lose things"—as if her son had been a misplaced, er, prescription).

The long preface concluded, here is what Rush Limbaugh said, crazily weaving in and out of the topic of Cindy Sheehan, in his broadcast of August 15. He even wanders back into football, and the very topic that proved his end at ESPN, Donovan McNabb of the Philadelphia Eagles (honestly, if he ever wanted to be analyzed, he would be such a juicy case that psychiatrists would bid for Limbaugh's rights). Limbaugh had wandered into this via the news of the withdrawal of the anti–John Roberts advertisement from NARAL:

They pulled this ad because it wasn't working. They didn't pull this ad because of a bite of conscience or, ooh, this is wrong. And their mistake was they're telling themselves they came out of the barn too soon with it. If they'd have come out of this say a week before September 6th. Well, stop and think about it. If they would have run this ad, if this would have started a week before September 6th, CNN carrying it, and none of the Democrats denouncing it, and without a whole lot of time to gin up, it would have probably had more effect. So I think they're going to learn from this that they didn't keep their powder dry, they just were too eager.

But the fact that they are too eager—I mean, Cindy Sheehan is just Bill Burkett. Her story is nothing more than forged documents, there's nothing about it that's real, including the mainstream media's glomming onto it, it's not real. It's nothing more than an attempt, it's the latest effort made by the coordinated left. And all of these efforts are bombing; they're all failing miserably, in and of themselves.

Now, this is not to say that all is rosy. I don't want you to misunderstand. But I don't get that worked up about it. I have an attitude about it. I've been sharing this with you for the longest time. So I think we're in a new era. The left doesn't get away with this stuff anymore. They're not getting away with it now. I know it's irritating, I know it's frustrating, I know it makes you mad, does me, too, but it's not helpful to the people who are doing this, it is not assisting them.

They are going to try to claim that Cindy Sheehan is responsible for the Bush poll numbers on Iraq being down, but those numbers were falling before Cindy Sheehan did this. I'm not saying the mainstream press isn't effective in certain areas anymore, I'm not saying the mainstream press doesn't have the ability to shape opinion. Just saying on this, this is not the thing everybody should be worried about. I don't have one in my mind that is, something everybody ought to be worried about, but if you're going to be angry at this, and I understand the anger, and I share some of it, too, the anger here, to me, is how the left and the media are trying to make this bigger than it is.

But that still takes me back to the fact that they know they're losing, they know they're losing big time. These people are throwing it up against the wall. It's the fourth quarter and all they're doing is throwing long bombs and their quarterback's gotten too tired to finish the game and their wide receiver is out there making all kinds of disparaging comments about the quarterback and getting kicked out of camp.

The situation with the Philadelphia Eagles pretty much dovetails what's going on with the Democratic Party right now if you ask me. It does. I don't think that we're looking at people who have a posture of confidence. This is not the kind of thing that winners do. It's all done in total desperation, as is the mainstream press's ability to prop it up.

What's she got? A hundred stragglers have showed up down there, a hundred peaceniks, a hundred long-haired, maggot-infested, dope-smoking FM types, essentially, are down there joining her. And if this were genuine, if this were like it was back in Vietnam—remember, that's what they're trying to turn this into. They're just reliving the old halcyon days of the anti-war movement in the sixties. They would have had hundreds of thousands of people down there. They would have had mass marches. There would have been the need for riot cops outside Bush's ranch down there. This is so obviously a desperation move.

Now, I don't have a whole lot of sympathy for the woman. I think she's taken the grieving process here to lengths that most people don't, and she's being fueled by all of this attention. But this is just a long way of saying I'm not—you can call about it and you can talk about it but I just am not that worked up about it because, to me, it's sort of like—I got an e-mail today from a guy said, "Rush, why aren't you talking about that radio scandal going on?" Why should I talk about it? Why should I talk about that, folks? There's a cardinal rule, when your enemy is destroying themselves, you shut up and you get out of the way and let them do it. And it's happening in countless areas and times on the left. Certain things you do need to give a little nudge, other things you just get out of the way.

But the longer the Sheehan thing goes on and the longer she's treated as some sort of super-celebrity by the press and the more outrageous things she says, trust me on this, the more people are going to get fed up with it. She's going to become the next Natalee Holloway before it's all said and done.

For sinking the worst to a new level . . .

Rush Limbaugh, *today's Honorary Worst Person in the World!*

Sharing Costs $19.99

Kicking off the nominees, Loew's Cineplex Theaters in Wallkill, New York. During a matinee of the new flick *March of the Penguins*, Anthony Patti was enjoying himself, laughing loudly, too loudly for the manager, who told his family that Anthony would have to leave. Anthony is 7. He's in a wheelchair. He has cerebral palsy and autism. The manager did say his family could stay if he left.

Nominated at the silver level, Snoop Dog. The rapper and fo' shizzle guy was nice enough to volunteer to coach kids' football in southern California's Orange County Conference, and then promptly started his own conference, the Snoop Youth Football League. The Orange County Conference accuses him of raiding it for players and coaches.

But the winner . . .

Amber Frey, Scott Peterson's former mistress. At the Learning Annex in San Francisco yesterday, she spoke to a group of women, saying she hoped to teach them how they could bounce back from adversity just as she did. She charged each woman $19.99 for her lecture. "I feel there's something I have to share, and I feel almost like I need to," she said. "They're questioning how I got through this to where I am today."

Part of the answer to that is, of course, by charging $19.99 each.

Amber Frey, *today's Worst Person in the World!*

We're Weary Too

There's just two this time:

Getting the silver in a very close race, Brent Bozell. Yes, the wacky guy from that Media Research Center scam accused me of distortion for having said that Rush Limbaugh had said on air, "Cindy Sheehan is just Bill Burkett. Her story is nothing more than forged documents. There's nothing about it that's real."

The only person distorting, as usual, is Bozell. Limbaugh said it on the air on August 15. We have the transcript. Nothing in the transcript mitigates what he said.

But the winner . . .

Limbaugh for saying "I never said this," when, of course, he sure did, especially considering that the line comparing Sheehan to Burkett was a featured quote on his Web site for his paying subscribers, until it was mysteriously scrubbed off.

And having now added about Sheehan's dead son, quote, "I'm weary of even having to express sympathy. We all lose things." Like your career, Rush. You're finished. Credibility spent. Get lost.

Once again . . .

Rush Limbaugh, *today's Worst Person in the World!*

Friends Don't Let Friends
Drive Drunk

AUGUST 22, 2005

Nominated at the bronze level, Wal-Mart, specifically, the Wal-Mart in Brownsville, Oregon. The home office guys have overruled the ones in Brownsville, Oregon. When a retired couple accidentally walked out of the store with 10 bags of manure priced at $1 each, the city accepted their explanation. They simply forgot to pay.

Wal-Mart did not. It demanded $175 in penalties or threatened suit against the couple. Given what was in the bags, this recalls the famous aphorism about "ten pounds of manure in a five-pound bag."

At the silver level, there's Matthew Flynn of West Hartford, Connecticut. That is an area in which tempers frequently run high over the music played by passing ice cream trucks. They've actually tried to legislate this. They need to. Police say Mr. Flynn was trimming his hedges last night when one of the trucks drove past, its jingles blaring out into the late summer Connecticut evening. And that's when he allegedly threatened to emasculate the ice cream man with his trimmer.

But the winner . . .

Darrell Johnson of Ottumwa, Iowa. Police there say that after a night out, his buddy, Jerry Miller, thought Darrell was too drunk to drive, so Jerry tried to pull Darrell out of his car. Friends don't let friends drive drunk.

That's when Darrell shot him.

Darrell Johnson, *today's Worst Person in the World!*

Pie Lady

AUGUST 23, 2005

First, there's the group Save the Newchurch Guinea Pigs, celebrating this evening after a British farm announced it would stop raising the animals for clinical testing. It and other groups have been attacking this company and this farm for seven years. Last year, somebody dug up the body of the dead grandmother of the owner. Nice.

Also nominated, an unnamed patient of Dr. Terry Bennett. He told her she was officially obese and really needed to lose weight to save her life. So she filed a complaint with New Hampshire's attorney general.

But the winner . . .

An old favorite here, Ann Coulter. In a recent column, she writes of terrorists, "It is far preferable to fight them in the streets of Baghdad than in the streets of New York, where the residents would immediately surrender." Ms. Coulter evidently did not know that most of 9/11 occurred in New York, New York, the city in which it's rather obvious that the residents never surrendered. This is from somebody who ran away in terror from a pie. Does this woman even live in this country?

Ann Coulter, *today's Worst Person in the World!*

Does he get visibly dumber as the hour wears on?

Revisit Your Commitment

SEPTEMBER 7, 2005

At the bronze level: Commander Michael Holdener, air operations chief at the Navy base at Pensacola. He chastised two of his helicopter pilots. They had come upon a hundred residents trapped in Katrina's floodwaters near the University of New Orleans and rescued them. But they weren't supposed to do that, says Commander Holdener. They were supposed to just deliver water and spare parts to Mississippi and then come right back.

They had a lot of nerve rescuing civilians during the return trip. There might have been more spare parts to ship.

Also nominated, the FEMA guy in charge of maps. Twice yesterday, medical teams were scrambled at the airport in Charleston, South Carolina, to meet a plane full of injured evacuees from Houston. Both times FEMA had sent the planes to Charleston, West Virginia.

But your winner . . .

FEMA spokesperson Mary Hudak. She has defended what the agency did with 1,400 firefighters from across the country who had volunteered to help throughout the Gulf Coast. FEMA told the firefighters that they would be handing out fliers with FEMA's toll-free phone number to residents, most of whom don't have working phones.

Some of the firemen went home. Ms. Hudak said that they needed to "revisit [their] commitment to FEMA, to firefighting, and to the citizens of this country." Hey, lady, I think we need to revisit your commitment.

Fifty of the firefighters were sent to Louisiana to stand next to the president during his tour of the afflicted areas.

FEMA spokesperson Mary Hudak, *today's*
Worst Person in the World!

Jumping the Shark

SEPTEMBER 8, 2005

As we began to get a full perspective of the federal disaster relief—or perhaps that would be better phrased "federal relief disaster"—an honorary Worst Person. It should be no surprise that criticism of the president, or the federal response, in the wake of the disaster that followed Hurricane Katrina, was initially portrayed as partisan pot-shotting. That is the default setting of our world, after all. We take sides on everything.

Well, except for 9/11, when Mr. Bush's approval rating was 90 percent and his disapproval, 6 percent. And also, except for right after Katrina, when the idea that only Liberals or political opportunists were being critical, was not just intuitively nuts—it was factually ludicrous.

Read this: The language is, to say the least, uncategorical. "Democrats have seized on the administration's performance in handling Katrina to bash George W. Bush," the nationally syndicated columnist writes. "But Republicans are not much happier with him. . . . When Republican House members participated in a telephone conference call September 1, the air was blue with complaints about the handling of Katrina . . . the GOP lawmakers were unhappy with their administration's performance."

That's from the September 8 column of Robert Novak's column—not exactly the work of a man known as a thorn in the administration's side.

For the president, it actually got worse. Many editorials in major newspapers were almost venomous toward Mr. Bush and the federal response. An excerpt from one: "Mayor Nagin's responses to this crisis, while flawed, have shown better leadership than both Governor Blanco's and President Bush's."

That's from the editorial in the *Manchester Union Leader* of Manchester, New Hampshire. That's the newspaper that has previously identified itself as the most conservative in the country. It has six national columnists: Novak, Jonah Goldberg, Charles

Krauthammer, Michelle Malkin, Deroy Murdock, and George Will. Not exactly a hotbed of commies.

And what it wrote about Mr. Bush was nothing compared to what it had written about him the previous Wednesday—decrying his decision to continue with his ordinary schedule "as if nothing important had happened the day before."

"A better leader," the paper continued on August 31, "would have flown straight to the disaster zone and announced the immediate mobilization of every available resource to rescue the stranded, find and bury the dead, and keep the survivors fed, clothed, sheltered and free of disease.

"The cool, confident, intuitive leadership Bush exhibited in his first term, particularly in the months following September 11, 2001, has vanished. In its place is a diffident detachment unsuitable for the leader of a nation facing war, natural disaster, and economic uncertainty."

That would be the president of the United States jumping the proverbial shark, and not doing it very successfully either.

George W. Bush, today's Honorary Worst Person in the World!

Surprisingly Still Employed

SEPTEMBER 13, 2005

Today, three Katrina-related nominees for the title of Worst Person in the World.

Nominated at the bronze level: John Stossel. The broadcaster writes an online column entitled "In praise of price gouging." He defends the guy who charges you twenty bucks for water for your dehydrated child because, if he'd kept the price down, he'd have already been sold out, and your child would die.

But by that logic, John, the price-gouger has also killed the other 177 children whose parents didn't have the twenty bucks.

Also, Louis Farrakhan. In North Carolina, he repeated the rumor going around that one of the levee breaches in New Orleans was no accident. Quoting him, "It may have been blown up to destroy the black part of town and keep the white part dry"; he added, "I heard from a very reliable source who saw a 25-foot-deep crater under the levee breach."

So this source saw this crater while the water was flowing into the city through the levee and over the crater? Who is he? Ray Milland, the Man with the X-Ray Eyes?

But the winner?

James Taranto of the *Wall Street Journal*'s Web page. You heard of the incident where a New Orleans evacuee swore, live, on Fox? And he compared the evacuation buses to the slave ships? Well, during this interview the guy was standing with a woman, maybe his wife, we don't know. He was black; she wasn't.

So on the *Wall Street Journal* web site, this Taranto guy runs a picture from the interview and writes below it, "Looks just like a slave ship, doesn't it? Well, except that on a slave ship, he probably wouldn't have his arm around a white woman."

Surprisingly enough still employed by the *Wall Street Journal* . . .

***James Taranto**, today's Worst Person in the World!*

It Should Be Called Negatronic

And three more Katrina-related nominees for the title of Worst Person in the World . . .

Nominated at the bronze level: Renee Holcombe, the now ex-Associate Vice President for Student Services at Greenville Technical College in South Carolina. In two separate briefings to her staff of about 40 last week, she explained that the college would be helping the city out with its New Orleans evacuees by sending some of its buses to pick up the children. She didn't call them "children," though. She called them "yard apes." Ms. Holcombe has resigned.

If we're lucky, from the country.

Also, the BMS Catastrophe Company of Fort Worth, Texas. It said it was willing to pay $7.50 an hour for 500 people to help with disaster relief cleanup in New Orleans, for at least six weeks. Kalila Dalton and Chris Tucker from Lawrence, Kansas, were on the bus to New Orleans when they found out they were being diverted to Biloxi, where their disaster relief work turned out to be cleaning up the Beau Rivage Casino. When they complained, they were told they could quit, but there was no transportation, and they risked being shot by the National Guard.

A well-named corporation, BMS Catastrophe.

But the winner . . .

John Gentry, President of Positronic Industries of Mount Vernon, Missouri. The Saturday before the hurricane hit, one of Mr. Gentry's employees, Barbara Roberts, went to her daughter's home in Columbia, Missouri, to babysit her granddaughter. Barbara's daughter and son-in-law were in New Orleans. They got trapped there. They were OK, but they couldn't get home to Missouri.

So in the crisis Barbara Roberts stayed in their home, taking care of her granddaughter, through the first Thursday after the hurricane. Ms. Roberts finally got back to work after taking five unpaid days off.

Whereupon, she got fired by . . .

John Gentry, *today's Worst Person in the World!*

Does He Get Visibly Dumber?

Today, three new Katrina-related nominees for the title of Worst Person in the World:

Nominated at the bronze level: Some of the evacuees. Yes, I'm blaming the victims. At least the ones that our NBC station in Houston is reporting have been using those FEMA and Red Cross debit cards at local strip clubs.
"I lost all my clothes, now you lose all yours."

Also, there's the U.S. Department of Justice. The newspaper the *Clarion-Ledger* of Jackson, Mississippi, has found an e-mail the DOJ sent to the various U.S. Attorneys' offices this week. It asks for them to contact the Department if any of them have defended "the Army Corps of Engineers against claims brought by environmental groups seeking to block or otherwise impede the Corps work on the levees in New Orleans."
In other words, the federal government is trying to find out if it can blame the environmental groups for the post-Katrina flooding.

But the winner . . .

The Big Giant Head, Bill O'Reilly. On the radio, saying, "I just wish Katrina had only hit the United Nations building, nothing else, just had flooded them out. And I wouldn't have rescued them," Bill evidently not realizing that if the UN, at 48th Street and First Avenue in New York City, got flooded out, there would be an excellent chance that Fox News, at 48th Street and Sixth Avenue in New York City, would also get flooded out and only the incredible supply of hot air he keeps in his lungs might keep him above water.
If you watch him, does he get visibly dumber as the hour wears on?

Bill O'Reilly, *today's Worst Person in the World!*

A Bill O'Reilly Glossary of Terms

Big Giant Head   Our original pseudonym for O'Reilly on *Countdown*. It is an arcane reference to the Supreme Leader in the old NBC sitcom *3rd Rock from the Sun*. The BGH was a figure of impossibly simultaneous terror and farce, who turned out to be played by William Shatner. Reference dropped in deference to Mr. Shatner.

Billo   The final pseudonym for O'Reilly on *Countdown*. This one was suggested by my radio (and former ESPN SportsCenter) partner Dan Patrick. It's perfect in many ways, not the least of which is the fact that it's a homonym for *billow*, a word whose definition reads, "A great swell, surge, or undulating mass, as of smoke or sound." That's Bill, ain't it?

Factor   Billo's own title for his own show. He treats it as if he invented the word, which, given his narrow world-view, he probably believes he did.

Factor **fiction**   Our title for any segment in which we translate one of his longer rants into English, such as the occasion in 2006 in which he claimed his April ratings had grown from the preceding April. In fact they had declined 3 percent, but he had managed to cook the books to count only those nights in which he "anchored The Factor." In ratings etiquette, this is a little akin to a baseball hitter saying that the only times at bat that counted toward his batting average were when he got hits.

fair and balanced   Fox News Channel's clever but fundamentally oxymoronic network slogan. "Balanced" means that a guest with a contrary viewpoint must appear in any discussion, even if the discussion is about in which direction the sun rises.

fair and balanced and dead   Our variation on the Fox slogan, especially as it pertains to O'Reilly's audience's age, whose average rose past the discouraging 70 mark in 2006.

fair and unbalanced   Our double-entendre version of the Fox slogan, implying a lack of not merely political "balance," but also of balance of the psychological kind.

falafel   Yes, it's a sandwich containing fried chickpeas. But more to the point, in the legal papers documenting Billo's conversations with ex-producer Andrea Mackris, it's his famous (and disturbing) slip of the tongue. He was describing which implement he wished to use to attend to a woman's body in a shower, and for a time accurately described same as a *loofah*. Suddenly and inexplicably (for your own sake, don't think about what could have distracted him), he began to call it a *falafel*. As I said to Jay Leno in a 2004 appearance on *The Tonight Show*: "If you can't tell the difference between your loofah and your falafel, what's the point of having a woman in your shower anyway?"

falafel fatwa   The work of our graphics/creative team at *Countdown* to describe Billo's unfortunate 2006 petition drive to have me fired and replaced by onetime MSNBC host Phil Donahue. Our entire staff, of course, signed the petition. So, apparently, did an "A. Mackrishasyour-money" of "Falafel, UT."

Fox not facts   Our own slogan for Fox News Channel. For some reason, Roger Ailes isn't interested.

Fox Security   The unfortunate individual or individuals who called at least two of the callers to Billo's radio show who mentioned my name (see "Say the Secret Word"). He/they really exist, but (and don't break this to Bill) they do not have police powers to arrest all those who disagree with his wisdom.

loofah   See "falafel"; also "Mackris, Andrea."

Mackris, Andrea   This is the woman who started the snowball of Billo's equanimity headed down the ski slope of his invulnerability. The former producer whom he allegedly regaled with unwanted "adult conversations" in a series of phone calls. He tried to preempt her sexual harassment lawsuit by filing one of his own, and wound up settling the matter by paying her what the *New York Daily News* reported was as much as $10 million. The notes of the conversations were so detailed that it was widely concluded Mackris must have recorded them. I offered $99,000 to settle her outstanding debts in exchange for the tapes, and viewers pledged another $50,000 or $60,000, but evidently (and correctly) she went for the higher offer. Billo announced the resolution by saying the story was over, to which I replied on the air, "*You* don't tell me when it's over, I tell *you* when it's over." It ain't over.

National Punting Championship   What Billo claimed to have won as a senior at Marist College in 1970, as he wrote of his exploits in a densely ego-packed essay inside the 2005 Super Bowl program. Given my sports background, I knew this was something I would've known about were it true, and I didn't. Billo wrote of winning the statistical competition "in my division." Turns out Marist didn't play intercollegiate football until 1978; the "division" O'Reilly played in was a loosely organized group of college "club" teams about one half step up from intramural or pickup games. In answer, he posted on his Web site an actual copy of the statistical record book for the 1970 season. It was mimeographed—which I think proved my point.

No-Spin Zone   That time of "The Factor" in which Billo spins three to four times as much as usual.

Papa Bear   Comedian and commentator Stephen Colbert's nickname for Billo.

say the secret word   Another *Countdown* catchphrase, coined after O'Reilly threatened a caller to his radio show with a visit from "Fox Security" and "local authorities," because he *said* the secret word, namely my name.

smear merchant   Billo's term for anybody who disagrees with him. Specifically Al Franken, Media Matters for America, me, or any of roughly 4,000,000,000 other people and organizations.

Sweet Jesus I Hate Bill O'Reilly   An early book (and subsequent Web site of the same name) chronicling the Billo canon.

Talking Points Memo   Billo's title for his opening remarks. Over a decade of programs, it has yet to dawn on him that the phrase has lost its original meaning of a series of bulletlike notes, and been transformed into the definition of political claptrap and parroted party spin.

Ted Baxter   Occasional *Countdown* pseudonym for Billo, plus the voice I impersonate when reading actual O'Reilly quotes. Also the only part of the entire O'Reilly experience that I regret, as it besmirches to some degree the memory of the great actor Ted Knight from *The Mary Tyler Moore Show*. But I am sure if Ted knew about Bill, he'd consent to the characterization.

Naming Rights

Nominated at the bronze level: The folks at IraqPartnership.Org. The 200 billion U.S. taxpayer dollars we've spent there, not enough. They want Americans to make contributions to the rebuilding. A British newspaper says that in about two weeks' time, those contributions have amounted to 600 bucks.

Also: Paul F. Weinbaum and Martin J. Boyd, two residents of greater Las Cruces, New Mexico. They've sued over three religious symbols on the official emblem of the city of Las Cruces: three crosses. See, "Las Cruces" in Spanish means *the crosses*.

But the winner:

Congressman Richard Pombo of California, the chairman of the House Resources Committee. He has proposed selling naming rights to many of our national parks and just plain selling as many as 16 of them to developers. One of them is the famous Theodore Roosevelt Island in the middle of the Potomac just outside D.C.

Congressman Pombo is a Republican. Evidently he doesn't know that Theodore Roosevelt was also a Republican.

*Congressman **Richard Pombo**, today's*
Worst Person in the World!

Everyone's Doing a Heckuva Job

SEPTEMBER 26, 2005

Also, some Honorary Worst Persons. Even his staunchest defenders had long since admitted that whatever else the president did or didn't do, or was or wasn't *supposed* to do, his supposedly solid political sense let him down completely at the beginning of the month of the hurricanes.

It had seemed to rebound lately. Until this day, anyway.

That's when a protestor was arrested on a technicality, not far from the White House. You might recognize her name: Cindy Sheehan. And, that's when it was revealed that FEMA had apparently rehired a former employee as a consultant. You might recognize his name, too: Mike Brown.

According to two congressional sources, at a meeting with staff of the special House committee looking into Katrina preparations, the disgraced and displaced former FEMA director said he had rejoined the agency as a consultant to "provide a review" of how the agency functioned before, during, and after the storm.

A congressional aide told NBC News nobody's *sure*, but it is assumed Brown is being *paid* by FEMA. He was to testify the next day before that House committee, prompting our colleague Howard Fineman to joke that only in Washington would a man on his way to the electric chair be *paid* to belt himself in.

But the timing—Brown's announcement to the staffers came just hours after the arrest of Sheehan in Washington for not having a permit to sit down rather than just march—suggests that the political tin ear was back in control at the White House.

The president doesn't *run* the District of Columbia police, of course—not even Karl Rove can claim that responsibility. But one would think, what with Hurricanes Katrina and Rita proving to the administration the wisdom of the old saw that it's truly an ill wind that blows no one any good, a message would've gone out. Something along the lines of: "don't touch Cindy Sheehan even if she self-immolates"—we finally just ended her publicity streak.

And one would've thought the FEMA folks would have been smarter than to let the face of the Katrina disaster, Mike Brown, back on to the public stage.

Karl Rove and the political geniuses at the White House, *today's Honorary Worst Persons in the World!*

You Say Nudge, I Say Noodge

SEPTEMBER 27, 2005

Nominated at the bronze level: Patriarch Alexei II, the head of the Russian Orthodox Church, who has just elevated a Russian military hero of the era of Napoleon. Admiral Fyodor Ushakov has been named the church's patron saint of long-distance Russian aircraft carrying nuclear weapons.

"Then lobbeth thou thy holy hand grenade . . ."

Also nominated: Alessandra Stanley, the notorious TV writer of the *New York Times*. Her paper finally gave up today and published an "editor's note" about when she wrote "Fox's Geraldo Rivera . . . nudged an Air Force rescue worker out of the way so his camera crew could tape him as he helped lift an older woman in a wheelchair to safety." The paper admits, "no nudge was visible on the broadcast."

But the winner . . .

Geraldo Rivera, who has made an absolute asinine jackass out of himself over this for the last 22 days. As the *Times* noted: "The editors understood the 'nudge' comment as a figurative reference." And, of course, there is the possibility Ms. Stanley was writing not the word "nudge" but the similarly spelled Yiddish word "noodge," a verb, defined as "to annoy persistently, pester."

Which, coincidentally, is also the dictionary definition you find when you look up . . .

Geraldo Rivera, *today's Worst Person in the World!*

The National Scold

Nominated at the bronze level: Scott Peterson. Yep, that guy. He is on death row, but it could be decades before he is executed, or has his sentence commuted in some way. His wife's insurance company, however, is ready to pay off on her quarter-of-a-million-dollar policy. And Peterson won't waive his rights to it.

Also nominated, Tennessee State Representative Stacey Campfield. He was rejected for membership in the Black Legislative Caucus possibly because he's a white guy. Odd enough, but then came Representative Campfield's bitter response to the rejection: "My understanding is," he said, "that the Ku Klux Klan doesn't even ban members by race."
Somebody voted for this dude.

But the winner . . .

The National Scold, Bill Bennett, talking on his radio show about recent economic theories suggesting that one of the reasons the crime rate has declined in the last 35 years is that abortion has been legalized. He said he found the following idea "impossible, ridiculous, and morally reprehensible," but "if you wanted to reduce crime you could . . . abort every black baby in this country, and your crime rate would go down."
Mr. Bennett, could you just go back to devoting your radio show to tips on how to win at high-stakes slots and video poker?

Bill Bennett, *today's Worst Person in the World!*

Blood Drive

Nominated at the bronze level: Mayor Marcos Irizarry of Lahas in Puerto Rico. The territory is in dire financial straits, the government asking its employees to voluntarily shorten their work weeks. But Mayor Irizarry thinks taxpayers should pay some of the $100,000 it will cost to set up a proposed landing strip in their city.

A landing strip for UFOs.

The runner-up: Major General Leif Simonsen, head of the Danish Air Force. His people have agreed to pay nearly $5,000 in damages to Olovi Nikkanoff, but they will not change any of their policies.

Mr. Nikkanoff is one of Denmark's many professional Santa Clauses. His territory is the island of Fyn. But last February, a Danish fighter jet made a low pass near Mr. Nikkanoff's farm, and the shock of the deafening noise proved just too much for one of Mr. Nikkanoff's Christmastime helpers. His reindeer. Named Rudolph.

That's right. The Danish Air Force killed Rudolph the Reindeer.

But the winner:

The promoters of NecroComicon, a comic and horror convention in the L.A. suburb of Northridge. The special celebrity guests this weekend are O.J. Simpson and Al Cowlings. Pose with O.J.'s arm around your shoulders and neck for only 95 bucks. Bad enough— but get this additional note from the press release: "The Red Cross is also scheduled to hold a *blood drive* at the event."

The promoters of NecroComicon, *today's*
Worst Persons in the World!

And then realized they
had a really bad public
relations nightmare
on their hands.

Ice Storm

Nominated at the bronze level: Boeing and Bell Helicopter. Advertising their new Osprey chopper in trade magazines by showing Special Forces Troops rappelling from them into something identified as the "Muhammed Mosque" with the caption "It descends from the heavens. Ironically it unleashes hell." The companies have apologized and may soon run an actual raid on their ad agency.

Also nominated: The mayor of Riviera Beach, Florida. Inspired perhaps by the Supreme Court, he wants to use eminent domain to displace about 6,000 local residents along the beach and build a $1 billion waterfront yachting and housing complex. Like this doesn't make him enough of a schmuck, the mayor's name is Michael Brown.

But the winner, speaking of which . . .

FEMA! As Lisa Myers reported, the agency bought $100 million worth of ice to be trucked to victims of Hurricane Katrina, only to learn that most of the area had enough ice. So they rerouted it around the country for days and weeks. Well, it's official now: a month after the storm hit, virtually all of the 182 million pounds of ice is back in government freezers in places as far away as Fremont, *Nebraska*.

After they used our tax dollars to take all that ice out for a drive.

***FEMA**, today's Worst Person in the World!*

The Student Is Now the Master

First up, there's Dr. Randall Smith of Gresham, Oregon. He's already gone to jail and lost his license for the cure he proposed for a woman patient complaining of lower back pain. Now she's suing him for $4 million. He said the pain would go away if she had sex with him.

And he probably planned to send her a bill, too . . .

Nominated at the silver level: Dave Worrell, spokesman for the Alaska Travel Industry Association, whose new billboards in L.A., Minneapolis, and Seattle promoting tourism to the 49th state show a big license plate with Alaska as the state name, and the tag that spells out "B 4 U DIE."

Thanks. Thanks for the reminder. How 'bout you guys visit New York before your next Alaskan earthquake?

But the winner . . .

Andrew Jacobs, a Vienna, Virginia, martial arts instructor. Among his pupils, a pair of 10-year-old twin girls. Saturday, police say, he went to their home, broke in, and tried to rob the house and abduct the girls. The bad news for Mr. Jacobs: he's a moron. Even though he was wearing a mask, the girls, of course, recognized his voice.

The good news for Mr. Jacobs: he is such a good martial arts instructor that the girls apparently beat the crap out of him, blackening his eye and giving their parents the chance to hit him over the head with a lamp.

Andrew Jacobs, *today's Worst Person in the World!*

Picture Perfect

At the bronze level: Ethan Orlinsky, general counsel for Major League Baseball. He is suing the Carver Academy of San Antonio, a school for 4- and 5-year-olds, nearly all of them on scholarship. Their logo is the interlocked initials "C.A.," which baseball claims is its exclusive property because it was the logo their team, the California Angels, used. Until 1996, when they changed the team name to the Anaheim Angels and then, this year, the Los Angeles Angels of Anaheim.

And they're suing the school to protect an out-of-date logo.

Also, Senator Ted Stevens of Alaska. He's managed to funnel $29 million in federal funding into the Alaska Fisheries Marketing Board and put his son on the board of directors. So when the board spent half a million to paint an Alaska Airlines plane to look like a big salmon . . . it was no big deal.

Hell, it wasn't their money. It was yours.

But the winner . . .

The folks at "Progress for America." Nobody begrudges the Conservative group setting up a Web site to get Harriet Miers confirmed for the Supreme Court. It's about this picture of the candidate on the home page of the site. They've touched it up to remove the bags under her eyes.

This is a 60-year-old Supreme Court nominee, guys, not Katie Holmes.

"Progress for America," today's Worst Persons in the World!

Iran County, Florida

At the bronze level: Principal Herman Allen of Gibbs High School in St. Petersburg. Twenty-five members of the Gibbs class of 1951, the class James Meredith graduated with, many of whom donated money to the new $47 million campus, wanted to take a tour of the place at ten o'clock last Friday morning during their class reunion. Principal Allen banned them from campus.

He said they posed a threat to the safety of the current students.

Nominated at the silver level: French designer Yvan Rodic. His new line of hooded sweatshirts has masks, some of them with fatigue coloring, just like the kind terrorists wear.

Moron.

But the winner . . .

The school board of Duval County, Florida. As part of the No Child Left Behind Act, public schools are supposed to hand personal information about all students to military recruiters unless a student's parents demand otherwise. But in Duval, if the student's parents demand otherwise, the school not only keeps the kid's personal information away from the recruiters, it also drops his or her name from sports scorecards and programs, the honor roll, and the yearbook.

Either/or. Either you let the military try to recruit your kid, or he doesn't get his picture in the yearbook.

I understand they do it that way in Iran, too.

The school board chairwoman says they're going to try to change the rule, but until then . . .

The Duval County Florida School Board, *today's Worst Persons in the World!*

The Farthest End of Foolishness

Our first posthumous nominee: Robert Prosser. Mr. Prosser, of Turtle Lake, Wisconsin, died in 2003. He was a collector. He left his four nieces and nephews half a dozen buildings in Turtle Lake. And every one of them is filled with his collection. He collected old telephones—750,000 of them. The executor of the estate thinks the collection is worth a million dollars.

His niece is looking for a landfill for it.

Also nominated: The commissioners of Cameron County, Texas. They have voted $24,000 of taxpayer money to restore a historic site in Brownsville, the bathroom in the courthouse. They'll make it look exactly as it did in 1912—93 years' worth of cleaning ago.

But the winner . . .

The staffers at the Wisconsin newspaper the *Fond du Lac Reporter*. In July it published an article about a gas station, complete with a photograph and address, formerly owned by a man it said a Department of Homeland Security agent had identified as "one of the plotters of the 9/11 terrorist attacks." What the agent had said was that the gas station owner was "an applauder of the 9/11 terrorist attacks."

The paper—surprise, surprise—has been sued.

Even so . . .

The staffers of the Fond du Lac Reporter, *today's Worst Persons in the World!*

We're Proud of What We've Accomplished; We've Just Begun

OCTOBER 11, 2005

Nominated at the bronze level: Richard Stephen "Bubba" Crosby. Crosby is the New York Yankees' spare part who started in center-field in last night's decisive playoff game against the Los Angeles Angels. The Yankees held a 2–1 lead in the second inning when Adam Kennedy of the Angels launched a fly ball toward right-centerfield. Crosby evidently did not consider the possibility that the Yankees also had a rightfielder in the game, named Gary Sheffield. They met—possibly for the first time—at full speed as both ran for Kennedy's hit. As they did an awful pirouette, the ball landed safely for a triple, two Angels runs, and, ultimately, the end of the Yankees' season.

And a rare two-fer: two Worsts in one story.

A high school senior in Kitty Hawk, North Carolina, doing home-work as part of a class project on freedom of dissent and the Bill of Rights, tacked a photo of the president to a wall. With the tack placed somewhere on the president's head. The student then took a photograph of the photo, with his own thumb in the frame, giving the thumbs-down. The student dropped off the roll of film to be developed at the photo department of the Kitty Hawk Wal-Mart. And they called the police, who in turn called the Secret Service.

Two Secret Service agents went to the high school, confiscated the picture of the picture, interviewed the student, interviewed the teacher, and threatened to turn the whole matter over to the local U.S. Attorney. And then realized they had a really bad public relations nightmare on their hands.

So the runner-up: the Secret Service.

But your winner . . .

The folks in the photo department of the Wal-Mart in Kitty Hawk, North Carolina, today's Worst Persons in the World!

We Report, You Decide

OCTOBER 11, 2005

And an honorary Worst to—well, it's so confusing, so eerie, so reeking of either paranoia or revelation that I don't even know who to give it to—beyond the good old amorphous, creepy Department of Homeland Security.

A week ago, I referred to the latest terror threat—the reported bomb plot against the New York City subway system—in terms of its timing. President Bush's speech about the war on terror had come earlier the same day, as had the breaking news of the possible indictment of Karl Rove in the CIA leak investigation. I suggested that in a three-year span there had been about 13 similar coincidences—a political downturn for the administration, followed by a "terror event"—a change in alert status, an arrest, a warning.

We figured we'd better put that list of coincidences on the public record. We did so on the television program, with ten of these examples. The other three are listed at the end of the main list, out of chronological order. The contraction was made purely for the sake of television timing considerations and permitted us to get the live reaction of the former undersecretary of homeland security, Asa Hutchinson.

We bring you these coincidences, reminding you, and ourselves, that perhaps the simplest piece of wisdom in the world is called "the logical fallacy." Just because Event A occurs, and then Event B occurs, that does not automatically mean that Event A *caused* Event B.

But one set of comments from an informed observer seems particularly relevant as we examine these coincidences. On May 10 of this year, after his resignation, former secretary of homeland security Ridge looked back on the terror alert level changes issued on his watch. Mr. Ridge said: "More often than not we were the least inclined to raise it. Sometimes we disagreed with the intelligence assessment. Sometimes we thought even if the intelligence was good, you don't necessarily put the country on (alert). . . . there were times when some people were really aggressive about raising it, and we said 'for that?'"

I'm not alone in wondering if this is paranoia or revelation. Please, judge for yourself.

Number One

May 18, 2002. The first details of the president's Daily Brief of August 6, 2001, are revealed, including its title: "Bin Laden Determined to Strike in U.S." The same day another memo is discovered, revealing that the FBI knew of men with links to Al Qaeda training at an Arizona flight school. The memo was never acted upon. Questions about 9/11 intelligence failures are swirling.

May 20, 2002. Two days later, FBI Director Mueller declares another terrorist attack "inevitable." The next day, the Department of Homeland Security issues warnings of attacks against railroads nationwide, and against New York City landmarks like the Brooklyn Bridge and the Statue of Liberty.

Number Two

June 6, 2002. Colleen Rowley, the FBI agent who tried to alert her superiors to the specialized flight training taken by Zacarias Moussaoui, whose information suggests the government missed a chance to break up the 9/11 plot, testifies before Congress. Senate Intelligence Committee Chair Graham says Rowley's testimony has inspired similar pre-9/11 whistle-blowers.

June 10, 2002. Four days later, speaking from Russia, Attorney General John Ashcroft reveals that an American named Jose Padilla is under arrest, accused of plotting a radiation-bomb attack in this country. Padilla had, by this time, already been detained for more than a month.

Number Three

February 5, 2003. Secretary of State Colin Powell tells the United Nations Security Council of Iraq's concealment of weapons, including 18 mobile biological weapons laboratories, justifying a UN or U.S. first strike. Many in the UN are doubtful. Months later, much of the information proves untrue.

February 7, 2003. Two days later, as anti-war demonstrations continue to take place around the globe, Homeland Security Secretary Ridge cites "credible threats" by Al Qaeda and raises the terror alert level to orange. Three days after that, Fire Administrator David Paulison—who would become the acting head of FEMA after the Hurricane Katrina disaster—advises Americans to stock up on plastic sheeting and duct tape to protect themselves against radiological or biological attack.

Number Four

July 23, 2003. The White House admits that the CIA—months before the president's State of the Union Address—expressed "strong doubts" about the claim that Iraq had attempted to buy uranium from Niger. On the 24th, the Congressional report on the 9/11 attacks is issued; it criticizes government at all levels; it reveals that an FBI informant had been living with two of the future hijackers; and it concludes that Iraq had no link to Al Qaeda. Twenty-eight pages of the report are redacted. On the 26th, American troops are accused of beating Iraqi prisoners.

July 29, 2003. Three days later, amid all of those negative headlines, Homeland Security issues warnings of further terrorist attempts to use airplanes for suicide attacks.

Number Five

December 17, 2003. 9/11 Commission Co-Chair Thomas Kean says the attacks were preventable. The next day, a federal appeals court says the government cannot detain suspected radiation bomber Jose Padilla indefinitely without charges, *and* the chief U.S. weapons inspector in Iraq, Dr. David Kay, who has previously announced he has found no weapons of mass destruction in Iraq, announces that he will resign his post.

December 21, 2003. Three days later, just before Christmas, Homeland Security again raises the threat level to Orange, claiming "credible intelligence" of further plots to crash airliners into U.S. cities. Subsequently, six international flights into this country are canceled after some passenger names purportedly produce matches on government no-fly lists. The French later identify those matched names: one belongs to an insurance salesman from Wales, another to an elderly Chinese woman, a third to a 5-year-old boy.

Number Six

March 30, 2004. The new chief weapons inspector in Iraq, Charles Duelfer, tells Congress we have still not found any WMD there. And, after weeks of refusing to appear before the 9/11 Commission, Condoleezza Rice finally relents and agrees to testify. On the 31st: Four Blackwater-USA contractors working in Iraq are murdered, their mutilated bodies dragged through the streets and left on public display in Fallujah. The role of civilian contractors in Iraq is widely questioned.

April 2, 2004. Homeland Security issues a bulletin warning that terrorists may try to blow up buses and trains, using fertilizer and fuel bombs—like the one detonated in Oklahoma City—stuffed into satchels or duffel bags.

Number Seven

May 16, 2004. Secretary of State Powell appears on *Meet the Press*. Moderator Tim Russert closes by asking him about the "enormous personal credibility" Powell had placed before the UN in laying out a case against Saddam Hussein. An aide to Powell interrupts the question, saying the interview is over. Powell finishes his answer, admitting that much of the information he had been given about weapons of mass destruction was "inaccurate and wrong, and, in some cases, deliberately misleading."

May 21, 2004. New photos showing mistreatment of Iraqi prisoners at Abu Ghraib Prison are released. On the 24th, Associated Press video from Iraq confirms that U.S. forces mistakenly bombed a wedding party, killing more than 40.

May 26 2004. Two days later, Attorney General Ashcroft and FBI Director Mueller warn that intelligence from multiple sources, in Ashcroft's words, "indicates Al Qaeda's specific intention to hit the United States hard," and that "90 percent of the arrangements for an attack on the United States were complete." The color-coded warning system is not raised, and Homeland Security Secretary Ridge does not attend the announcement.

Number Eight

July 6, 2004. Democratic presidential candidate John Kerry selects Senator John Edwards as his vice presidential running mate, producing a small bump in the election opinion polls and a huge swing in media attention toward the Democratic campaign.

July 8, 2004. Two days later, Homeland Secretary Ridge warns of information about Al Qaeda attacks during the summer or autumn. Four days after that, the head of the U.S. Election Assistance Commission, DeForest B. Soaries Jr., confirms he has written to Ridge about the prospect of postponing the upcoming presidential election in the event it is interrupted by terrorist acts.

Number Nine

July 29, 2004. At their party convention in Boston, the Democrats formally nominate John Kerry as their candidate for president. As in the wake of any convention, the Democrats dominate the media attention over the ensuing weekend.

Monday, August 1, 2004. The Department of Homeland Security raises the alert status for financial centers in New York, New Jersey, and Washington to Orange. The evidence supporting the warning—reconnaissance data, left in a home in Iraq—later proves to be roughly four years old and largely out-of-date.

Number Ten

October 6, 2005. At 10 A.M. eastern standard time, the president addresses the National Endowment for Democracy, once again emphasizing the importance of the war on terror and insisting his government has broken up at least ten terrorist plots since 9/11.

At 3 P.M. eastern time, five hours after the president's speech has begun, the Associated Press reports that Karl Rove will testify again to the CIA leak grand jury, and that Special Prosecutor Fitzgerald has told Rove he cannot guarantee that he will not be indicted.

At 5:17 P.M. eastern time, seven hours after the president's speech has begun, New York City officials disclose a bomb threat to the city's subway system—based on information supplied by the federal government. A Homeland Security spokesman says that the intelligence upon which the disclosure is based is "of doubtful credibility." And it later proves that New York City had known of the threat for at least three days and had increased police presence in the subways long before making the announcement at that particular time. A local New York television station, WNBC, reports it had the story of the threat days in advance but was asked by "high ranking federal officials" in New York and Washington to hold off its story.

Less than four days after revealing the threat, Mayor Michael Bloomberg says, "Since the period of the threat now seems to be passing, I think over the immediate future, we'll slowly be winding down the enhanced security."

While news organizations ranging from the *New York Post* to NBC News quote sources who say there was reason to believe that the informant who triggered the warning simply "made it up," a senior U.S. counterterrorism official tells the *New York Times*: "There was no there, there."

The list of three additional examples follows.

Number Eleven

October 22, 2004. After weeks of Administration insistence that there are terrorist plans to disrupt the elections, FBI, Law Enforcement, and other U.S. intelligence agencies report they have found no direct evidence of any plot. More over, they say, a key CIA source who had claimed knowledge of the plot has been discredited.

October 29, 2004. Seven days later—four days before the presidential election—the first supposedly new, datable tape of Osama Bin Laden since December 2001 is aired on the Al Jazeera network. A Bush-Cheney campaign official anonymously tells the *New York Daily News* that from his campaign's point of view, the tape is "a little gift."

Number Twelve

May 5, 2005. Eighty-eight members of the United States House of Representatives send a letter to President Bush demanding an investigation of the "Downing Street Memo"—a British document that describes the purported American desire dating to 2002 to "fix" the evidence to fit the charges against Iraq. In Iraq over the following weekend, car bombings escalate. On the 11th, more than 75 Iraqis are killed in one.

May 11, 2005. Later that day, an instructor and a student pilot violate restricted airspace in Washington, D.C. It is an event that happens hundreds of times a year, but this time the plane gets to within three miles of the White House. The Capitol is evacuated; Vice President Cheney, the First Lady, and Nancy Reagan are all rushed to secure locations. The president, biking through woods, is not immediately notified.

Number Thirteen

June 26, 2005. A Gallup poll suggests that 61 percent of the American public believes that the president does not have a plan in Iraq. On the 28th, Mr. Bush speaks to the nation from Fort Bragg: "We fight today because terrorists want to attack our country and kill our citizens, and Iraq is where they are making their stand. So we'll fight them there, we'll fight them across the world, and we will stay in the fight until the fight is won."

June 29, 2005. The next day, another private pilot veers into restricted airspace, the Capitol is again evacuated, and this time, so is the president.

To summarize, coincidences are coincidences. We could probably construct a similar timeline of terror events and warnings, and their relationship to the opening of new Wal-Marts around the country. Are these coincidences signs that the government's approach has worked because none of the announced threats ever materialized? Are they signs that the government has not yet mastered how and when to inform the public?

Is there, in addition to the "fog of war" a simple, benign "fog of intelligence"?

But, if merely a reasonable case can be made that any *one* of these juxtapositions of events is more than just coincidence, it underscores the need for questions to be asked in this country—questions about what is prudence, and what is fearmongering; questions about which is the threat of death by terror, and which is the terror of threat.

The Department of Homeland Security, today's Honorary Worst Persons in the World!

Balls

At the bronze level: Sylvester Stallone. A British tabloid reports he's agreed to star in *Rocky 6*. That's where the now 60-year-old Rocky Balboa comes out of retirement to fight bladder-control issues.

Nominated at the silver level: Ian Pearson, a "futurologist" with BT Laboratories in Great Britain. He sees a merger of two technologies: MP3 players and breast augmentations. The MP3 chip could sit inside the implant, while a signal could be relayed to headphones, with the whole rig controlled with a remote.
  "Hey! Those are NOT click wheels!"

But the winner . . .

Our friends at NASA. The result of the "Deep Impact" experiment, when they crashed the spacecraft into the Comet Tempel 1? Comets are actually "icy dirtballs." They are not, as previously believed, "dirty snow-balls."
  For this we paid $330 million?

NASA, *today's Worst Persons in the World!*

Omar Shamshoon

At the bronze level: New York radio hosts Mike Francessa and Christopher Russo. They complained that the New York Yankees did not provide free food for the reporters who went to the ballpark yesterday to interview Yankees players who were packing their stuff and going home for the winter.

As the late Howard Cosell paraphrased FDR's "Four Freedoms" into the "Four Freedoms for Sports Reporters": "freedom of admission, freedom of transportation, freedom of beverages, freedom of food."

The runner-ups, also from radio: George Lindsey, Lynda Lambert, and Aaron Miller, the morning team from WMXA in Louisville. They reported that a science experiment had gone horribly wrong, and a kitten named Skittles was now flying loose over the city in a basket tied to helium balloons. Uncounted anguished residents spent the day looking in vain for Skittles the Kitten in the skies above Louisville.

It was a prank. The morning team has been suspended, may be fired.

But the winner?

Michel Costandi, business development director of the Arab satellite TV network, MBC. "M" as in Michel. He has bought the rights to broadcast *The Simpsons* in Arabia. But to make it more "accessible" to the audience, he's not only dubbed it into Arabic, he's edited out all the bar scenes, changed the name Homer Simpson to Omar Shamshoon, stopped his beer drinking, and renamed his son Bart, Badr.

A lot of Arabs are offended. Why not just spend the money making a series about a real Arab family? Others, already fans of the "real" Simpsons, like a professor at Cal State–Stanislaus, said the hybrid version was "just painful—just drop the project, and air reruns of Tony Danza's show instead!"

Michel Costandi, *today's Worst Person in the World!*

The Astronomer Who Discovered
a Web Page

OCTOBER 17, 2005

Nominated at the bronze level: Mr. J. B. S. and his wife, Wendy, of London. Last week there appeared on a bridge a bedsheet on which was written: "Wendy, I want a divorce, J.B.S." Three days later, a new bedsheet appeared in the same place. It read, "No way, you are the cheat! Wendy."

Kids, that phrase "airing your dirty laundry" is not meant to be taken literally.

Also: Sri Lankan Airlines. You might want to skip them the next time you're thinking of traveling to the capital city of Colombo. For the third time in six weeks, one of their flights has been affected by a bomb threat. The latest one, authorities have discovered, was phoned in by a Sri Lankan Airlines flight attendant who wanted the day off.

But the winner . . .

Spanish astronomer Jose Luis Ortiz, who announced he and some colleagues had discovered a new planetoid in the Kuiper Belt. In fact, what they'd discovered was that astronomer Michael Brown of Cal Tech had discovered the new planetoid. And that he, Ortiz, had just made the announcement before Brown could. They'd found out what Brown had been looking at using a telescope in Chile. They did that by using Google to find copies of some of Brown's notes.

The astronomer who discovered a web page . . .

Jose Luis Ortiz*, today's Worst Person in the World!*

Think, Don McNulty

OCTOBER 18, 2005

The bronze goes to either Penn State women's basketball coach Rene Portland or her former player Jennifer Harris. Only the courts will decide. The coach berated the player last week, saying she had a poor attitude and work ethic. The player says none of that's true, that the coach is just avenging herself against her. The player says the coach harassed her, assuming she was gay, and when the player complained, the coach made the remarks about the work ethic. Punchline: player Harris says, by the way, she's not gay.

But her lawyer is from the National Center for Lesbian Rights.

Also nominated, an unnamed convict in Romania. Convicted on murder charges, he has filed a suit for contract violation. Against God. Says his baptism was a contract to keep him out of the hands of the devil, and obviously God didn't fulfill his end of the bargain.

But the winner . . .

Don McNulty, the founder of Bio Cleaning Services of America. Now advertising his services on a billboard on I-70 in St. Louis. The billboard features, in big letters, the words "Homicide," "Suicide," and "Death Cleaning." Mr. McNulty explains to the *St. Louis Post-Dispatch* that most property owners don't realize until it's too late that they're responsible for cleaning up a bloody, gory death. So he will do it for you.

Don't forget, for your next violent crime, think:

Don McNulty, *today's Worst Persons in the World!*

The Going Rate of a Soul

Bronze: Jirra Ware, an Australian insurance broker. He was such an alcoholic that he had a deal with his own bosses that he just wouldn't come back from lunch on Fridays because he was too drunk. He'd make up the work on the weekends.

They gave him time off to see a shrink every other week. But it didn't work out, and they let him go. So he sued them, claiming he had been discriminated against for having attention deficit disorder.

An Aussie court has just awarded Mr. Ware $10,000.

Also nominated: The Living Proof Christian Broadcasters. Five years ago, the folks who run the school's FM radio station at Maynard High in suburban Boston asked permission to increase its signal power from 10 watts to 250. As soon as it did that, that made their frequency, 91.7 FM, open to anybody who wanted to apply for it and who could convince the FCC that they'd better serve the public. The FCC has revoked the school's license and given it to . . . Living Proof Christian Broadcasters.

"Christian" obviously just a brand name there . . .

But the winners . . .

Sinclair Broadcast Group. The right-wing nuts—sorry, the TV station owners—last year, they fired their own Washington news bureau chief, Jon Leiberman, because he objected to Sinclair's effort to dress up the Swift Boat ad guys' attacks on John Kerry as a news documentary.

Last May, Sinclair objected when Leiberman got a journalism award. Now, Sinclair has sued Leiberman, seeking $17,000 in damages. Seventeen grand.

Y'know, boys, it is gonna take you more than seventeen grand to buy your souls back from the devil.

Sinclair Broadcast Group, *today's*
Worst Persons in the World!

The Most Confusing Parking Sign

OCTOBER 20, 2005

The bronze goes to Punji-lal, the 75-year-old mystic seer of the dusty village of Sabra, India. His latest prediction: that between 3 and 5 P.M. local time today, he'd die. At 5:01, he revised it to say he'd die fifteen years from now.

Runner-up: Political activist D. A. King, who spoke out against illegal immigration at a well-attended rally in Atlanta as 14 other protestors carried signs. Turns out the 14 other protestors were homeless people to whom King paid ten bucks apiece. But King says they agreed with him. "Trust me, they are angry . . . when the day comes when I cannot pay an American for an hour's worth of work for making their voices heard, it's a sad day."

As the Rutles sang, D. A., "All you need is cash."

But the winner . . .

Tom Walsh, city traffic engineer of Madison, Wisconsin, who put up a parking sign on Monroe Street that says "No Parking 5:30 P.M.–4 P.M." in apparent violation of the laws of physics and time! Apart from the fact that you also can't park between 4 P.M. and 5:30 P.M.

This beats out the old sign outside Winooski, Vermont, which read "Begin No Parking Here" for the title of most confusing parking sign on the continent.

Tom Walsh, *today's Worst Person in the World—between 5:30 P.M. and 4 P.M.!*

We're Still Paying for Him

At the bronze level: The two gun-wielding men who burglarized a donut shop in Everett, Washington. They were dressed as clowns. In full clown makeup. They are now being pursued by the group Insane Clown Posse.

At the silver level: The unnamed meter maid in Maroondah, Australia. She ticketed a parked car in that city, noticing the license plate, the make, and the violation, but not the body of the dead guy slumped over the steering wheel.

But your winner . . .

Brownie! Former FEMA director Michael Brown. You may remember the national shock when it was revealed that after his performance in New Orleans, he was still on the FEMA payroll, given 30 more days to get documents together for the post-Katrina FEMA postmortem. Guess what. He needed more time. So he's been given another 30-day contract.

We're *still paying for him*. How can we miss you if you won't go away? You know what? The president was right. Brownie, you are doing a heckuva job.

Michael Brown, *FEMA director emeritus, today's Worst Person in the World!*

Spanking Bill

OCTOBER 24, 2005

The bronze goes to the inimitable Department of Homeland Security. It has awarded a grant of $36,300 to the Kentucky State Office of Charitable Gaming. Thirty-six grand of our money to be spent keeping terrorists from raising money by playing bingo in Kentucky.

The runner-up, in a close race, Ann Coulter, who told her audience at a Republican fundraiser last Thursday in Gainesville, Florida, that the Iraq war was a "magnificent success." And, she added, "Frankly, I'm not a big fan of the First Amendment."

A reporter for a University of Florida newspaper noted, "The Republicans got in the spirit of the night while enjoying an SUV-size trailer full of Budweiser beer." Hell, if I had had to listen to that crap I would have too. . . .

But the winner . . .

Ohhhhhh! He's baaaack. The Big Giant Head again, explaining to his radio audience that we won the Second World War because of spanking.

"In the Great Depression," he said, "every American got spanked. And those Americans went to war during World War Two and won the very intense conflict and showed bravery across the broad, the Greatest Generation. The Greatest Generation, almost down to the man, was spanked, 'cause that's the way we did it in America. OK?"

Do you get the feeling he's about four minutes away from being committed?

Bill O'Reilly about spanking. Hey? Can we call Andrea Mackris?

Bill O'Reilly, *today's Worst Person in the World!*

One of the Greatest Pitchers of All Time

OCTOBER 24, 2005

An honorary *Worst:* baseball pitching ace Roger Clemens.

He's day-to-day. We're *all* day-to-day. Certainly his Houston Astros are.

I apologize—in making my World Series forecast (White Sox, possibly in a sweep, and it seems to me I mentioned how Phil Garner should've used relief star Brad Lidge in the last game against the St. Louis Cardinals and *not* waited to see if he'd give up another game-losing homer in his next appearance, in the Series)—I forgot to mention what I believe I noted on the radio or at least in an interview or two, namely, the ultimate effect of the Albert Pujols home run—that it would force Roy Oswalt to pitch again in the series against St. Louis and force the Astros to instead open with Clemens in Chicago.

That was particularly relevant because, as I did predict elsewhere, it meant that something would cause Roger Clemens to bail out of Game One.

You protest, in controlled agony. "Roger Clemens is one of the greatest pitchers of all time!" I giggle. "He is 12-and-7 lifetime in the post-season." I laugh. "He is undefeated over the course of six different World Series!" I do a spit-take.

Saturday's "hamstring pull" and the resultant exit after 54 pitches should've been predictable to the degree that the odds among the exotic wagerers of Vegas should not have exceeded 3:1 against.

Here is the nasty truth. After Saturday night, Roger Clemens has now made 33 post-season starts in the last two decades (an admittedly remarkable achievement). His team has lost 17 of them.

In the post-season, he is a sub-.500 starter.

To be fair, Saturday's loss only brought his team's record with him pitching *down* to .500 (4-4). But behind the simple numbers, he has an unfortunate resume of either coughing up leads his mates have given him (eight different games so far, in one of which in 2002 he blew three *separate* leads), or getting out of the game prematurely or controversially, or all of the above. If the Astros live to a Game Five and Clemens is healthy, they should just say, "No, thanks."

Let's start by acknowledging that you didn't *imagine* his occasional brilliance in the post-season. The Rocket pitched a five-hit 3–0 shutout into the ninth in his first short-rest start ever (against the Angels in Game Four of the 1986 ALCS, then he and Calvin Schiraldi blew it). He pitched seven particularly fine post-season games for the Yankees (most notably the 1999 World Series clincher, just two days after a shouting match with a fan outside the players' entrance at Yankee Stadium, and his 15-strikeout and 9-strikeout performances against the Mariners and the Mets in 2000). And the relief effort against the Braves in this year's Division Series—though it is of course not considered one of his starts—was an impressive three-inning performance.

On the other hand, though the quick exit, stage right, against the White Sox was quick, it was hardly atypical. How many "great" pitchers carry the baggage of six controversies or injuries?

1. 1990 ALCS Game Four at Oakland. The A's have already scored a run off him in the second inning when Clemens puts two men on—the second, by walking Willie Randolph. He then begins to shout loudly. "I thought Roger was swearing at me," said A's batter Mike Gallego. In fact, he's swearing at home plate umpire Terry Cooney—and if his post-game denial that he remembers any of it is correct, he may be doing so in a trancelike state. Cooney ejects Clemens, who makes contact with at least two other umpires during the subsequent argument. The A's score both runners, the Red Sox lose 3–1 and are swept.

2. 1999 ALCS Game Two at Boston. Red Sox fans, mistakenly believing Clemens jilted them to go to Toronto as a free agent when the move was largely the fault of Boston management, serenade the now-Yankee with a sing-song of "Rahh-jer, Rahh-jer." Rahhjer gives up five in the first (I was there, and I still don't believe I saw Jose Offerman triple off him and John Valentin homer off him) and lasts only through the first batter of the third inning. The Yankees lose 13–1 (their only post-season loss that

year). I was the dugout reporter during that game and none of my Yankee contacts would say a thing about why Clemens came out, until, in the seventh inning, David Cone finally explains: "He said he had a bad back." To this point, the record of Clemens's team in his 11 post-season starts is 3-and-8.

3. 2000 World Series Game Two at Yankee Stadium. Clemens is stunning—striking out nine Mets and giving them just two hits over eight innings. But if it had been Terry Cooney umpiring the plate and not Charlie Relaford (or, as Clemens would quaintly call him afterward, "Umpire Charlie"), Clemens could've easily been ejected again—early. This is the game in which he throws the piece of Mike Piazza's shattered bat more or less in Piazza's general direction. Again I'm the Yankee dugout reporter for this game, and coach Lee Mazzilli offers the following explanation for the incident: "I can't even imagine why he did that."

4. 2001 ALDS Game One at Yankee Stadium. Clemens gives up solo runs to Oakland in the first and fourth. Pitching to the first hitter in the fifth, he begins twitching. Joe Torre comes to the mound. Clemens, it turns out, has pulled a hamstring. Yanks lose 5–3.

5. 2003 ALCS Game Seven at New York. Clemens is battered by the Red Sox for six hits and four runs in three innings and leaves the most important game of the season down 4–0. The crash will be obscured by the unlikely relief pitching of Mike Mussina and the even more unlikely pennant-winning home run of Bret Boone.

6. 2005 World Series Game One at Chicago. Clemens has no control, is lucky to give up just three runs and four hits in his 54-pitch labor over two innings. He walks easily off the field after the second inning, but when he reaches the dugout steps, he begins to limp spectacularly. He has pulled another hamstring.

And just so you don't think I'm making that stat up—*eight* blown leads—here they are, too. This is, in short, not Christy Mathewson or Bob Gibson. This is a guy with a post-season record slightly less impressive than that of his journeyman teammate Russ Springer.

1. 1986 World Series Game Six at New York. The Red Sox give him a 2–0 lead, but Clemens gives it back. Boston scores again, and he leaves after seven, leading ahead 3–2. Then Schiraldi, Bob Stanley, and Bill Buckner happen.

2. 1988 ALCS Game Two at Boston. Given another 2–0 lead, Clemens surrenders a two-run homer by Jose Canseco and a Mark McGwire RBI in the seventh, and the Red Sox lose 4–3.

3. 1995 ALDS Game One at Cleveland. Again, it's 2–0 Boston, but the Indians, paced by an Albert Belle double, score three off him in the sixth. After Clemens leaves, the Red Sox rally to tie, only to lose on Tony Pena's homer in the thirteenth.

4. 2000 ALDS Game One at Oakland. Clemens is given *another* 2–0 lead by Yankees, gives it back in the fifth. The A's score their lead run on his wild pitch and add another in the sixth. The Yanks lose 5–3.

5. 2002 ALDS Game One at New York. Against the Angels, Clemens blows a 1–0 lead, then a 3–1 lead, then a 4–3 lead. They have rallied to tie it again as he leaves after the seventh, and ultimately win without him, 8–5.

6. 2004 NLCS Game Seven at St. Louis. The Astros give Clemens *another* 2–0 lead. He gives one back in the third, then an RBI double to Pujols and a two-run homer to Scott Rolen in the sixth. The Cardinals eliminate the Astros 5–2.

7. 2005 NLDS Game Two at Atlanta. Clemens is given a 1–0 lead; gives up five earned in five, including a three-run homer to rookie Brian McCann. Astros lose 7–1.

8. 2005 NLCS Game Three at Houston. Clemens is given yet another 2–0 lead, gives it back. As he is pinch hit for in the sixth, the Astros rally for two more and he gets credit for the 4–3 victory over St. Louis. His teams have now managed to win exactly *half* of his post-season starts—and two of the eight games in which he's coughed up leads.

Roger Clemens, *today's Honorary Worst Person in the World!*

To Get Girls

The bronze goes to Senate Majority Leader Bill Frist. That whole scandal about his "blind trust" selling off stock in his family hospital company just before the stock tanked? Turns out the only "blind trust" was ours, in his word. The asset-managers were required to notify Frist—and the Senate—anytime it sold or bought stocks for him. *The Washington Post* has copies of 15 of their letters to Frist since 2001.

Well, not a blind trust, so much as a nearsighted one.

The runner-up? Attorney Jerry Stewart of Benton, Arkansas. Appealing his second conviction for drunk driving, he showed up to court intoxicated.

And the winner?

Brian Jackson of Brentwood, Pennsylvania, ordered to pay a fine of $300 for impersonation. To get girls, he pretended he was Pittsburgh Steelers' starting quarterback Ben Rothlisberger, *and* former Steelers' back-up quarterback Brian Saint Pierre.

Here he's pretending he's a quarterback for the Steelers, who have three healthy quarterbacks when the New York Jets are 2-and-5 and their first-, second-, and third-string quarterbacks are all hurt.

Brian Jackson, *today's Worst Person in the World!*

Totally Supporting the Troops

Taking the bronze: An unnamed doctor at South Tyneside District Hospital in England. A woman named Paula Dadswell waited there for a doctor for two hours with her son, who was suffering bad cramps. Finally, one showed up. On a unicycle. He'd been riding up and down the ward on a unicycle.

The runner-up: Mark Barondess, a consultant to a group called the Pharmaceutical Research and Manufacturers of America. They figured they had to do something to thwart all those drugs coming in from Canada over the Internet. So they hired a publishing firm and a series of authors to write a novel called *The Karasik Conspiracy*, in which terrorists conspire to kill thousands of Americans . . . by poisoning the medicine coming in from Canada over the Internet.

But the winner . . .

Clark Galloway, vice president of operations of Benefit Management Administrators Inc. of Caledonia, Michigan. One of the company's receptionists, Suzette Boler, took four days off— unpaid—to say goodbye to her husband, Army Specialist Jerry Boler, before he shipped out to Iraq. When she got back, Benefit Management Administrators fired her.

"We gave her sufficient time to get back to work," Mr. Galloway told the *Grand Rapids Press*, and then added, "We are totally supportive of our troops and anything that is necessary to equip them and to encourage them as a company."

Yep, anything except not firing their wives as they ship out to Iraq.

Clark Galloway, VP of Benefit Management Administrators Inc. of Caledonia, Michigan, today's Worst Person in the World!

Do you wonder if he
worries about what
his job is going
to be, in hell?

Gilead Is the Balm

The bronze winner: Elaine Chao, your U.S Secretary of Labor. The department made a deal with Wal-Mart. In the event it wants to inspect a Wal-Mart for child labor violations, it has to give the company 15 days' notice.

The runner-up: Iyad Abu El Hawa, the owner of Comfort & Caring Home Health in Houston. Under arrest after giving flu shots to 14 senior citizens that turned out to contain zero percent vaccine and 100 percent distilled water.

The company is also alleged to have given the shots to 1,000 employees at an Exxon-Mobil company fair.

But the winner is . . .

Secretary of Defense Donald Rumsfeld. Speaking of the flu, you've heard of Tamiflu, the supposed best defense if the bird flu breaks out? In the president's new $7 billion bird flu plan, up to a billion of that could be spent buying Tamiflu. That's driven the stock price of Gilead Sciences, which makes the drug, from 35 bucks a share to 47 bucks a share.

Who used to be the *chairman* of Gilead Sciences? Who— though he's recused himself from decisions involving it—still owns between $5 million and $25 million worth of the company?

*Who else but **Donald Rumsfeld**, today's
Worst Person in the World!*

A Mother Load of Semen

NOVEMBER 3, 2005

The bronze winner: Rolf Evans, the Casualty Affairs Officer at Fort Lewis in Washington state. He's the civilian in charge of deciding which funeral homes handle the bodies of dead servicemen back from Iraq.

He's been arrested. Police say he was demanding kickbacks from the funeral homes.

The runner-up: Tom Benson, the owner of football's New Orleans Saints. Apart from his near constant threat to move the franchise permanently out of the crippled city, now he says there is no security in the stadium in Baton Rouge, the Saints' temporary home. He claims he could've been killed, so he won't go back there.

The nonstop booing Benson has been getting has, of course, nothing to do with that decision.

But the winner is . . .

Eric Fleming of Smithsburg, Maryland. Now this is awarded with some reluctance because he is the victim of a big-scale crime. He's out $75,000. Somebody stole his 70-pound tank full of bull semen.

That's right, another report of bull-semen rustling.

So why are we blaming the victim? Because of the message Mr. Fleming posted on his Web site after the theft. "I will give a nice fat reward for any information on semen that was stolen from my tank today. It was a mother load of semen."

Thanks for sharing that.

Eric Fleming, *today's Worst Person in the World!*

You Vote, We Pay

NOVEMBER 4, 2005

Bronze winner: Kevin Federline. Again. Yesterday we played for you some of his new rap song, which is so bad that it makes dogs yowl. Well, we forgot to point out that in it, he makes the verbal equivalent of a typo. We believe he meant to refer to *paparazzi* when he sang:

> I'm starin' in your magazines now every day and week . . .
> But maybe baby you can wait and see . . .
> Until then all these *Pavarottis* followin' me.

Our runner-up, and we've got two on a match here: Former House Majority Leader Tom DeLay. The Web site Political Money Line posts congressional ethics documents that indicate that a month ago, just after his indictment, DeLay accepted a free trip from Houston to Washington to make an appearance for the company paying for the trip. It cost $13,998.55.

A round-trip from Houston to D.C. For fourteen grand.

Who would've paid such an exorbitant figure just to get Tom DeLay back to Washington over the first weekend in October?

Who else but our winners . . .

The Fox News Channel! *Today's Worst Persons in the World!*

A Sticky Situation

NOVEMBER 4, 2005

The odds are fairly good you heard this on the news or some gaudy disc jockey told you about it or some unmarried male friend ran up to you, panting and seeming in fear of his life. It's the Ken Slabby story. The guy whose ex-girlfriend glued his privates to his stomach, then sealed up his derriere. Or as Gerry Rafferty and Stealers Wheel sang, "Stuck in the Middle with You."

Now Ken Slabby, of Pittsburgh, who's walking pretty well, wants $30,000 in damages from his ex-girlfriend, the aptly named Gayle O'Toole. Here's why.

After their relationship ended five years ago, according to Mr. Slabby, Ms. O'Toole tried to rekindle the friendship by inviting him over to her house, even though he was going to get married to somebody else. He fell asleep there, drugged, he says. And while he was unconscious, she used superglue to attach his penis to his stomach, his testicles to his leg and his buttocks to each other. She then poured nail polish on his head before waking him up and kicking him out of the house.

He had to walk, if you want to call it that, a mile to a convenience store to call for help. Once he got to the hospital, nurses actually had to peel the glue off his body parts.

Ms. O'Toole does not deny that she did any of these things. She just says it was consensual. That as part of their sex game, she used nail polish to paint sideburns on Mr. Slabby, in honor of Elvis. That he actually woke up and laughed about it. She didn't share what the superglue might have been in honor of. She even brought her own star witness to her strange sex life with Mr. Slabby. Her daughter took the stand yesterday in Ms. O'Toole's defense, saying, "I believe it was part of their relationship. That's all I can really say."

"Hi, Mom, where's Ken?" "I don't know, dear, he's late. He must be stuck in traffic."

While the courts try to make the best of a sticky situation, what, we asked, can you do with a pair like that? People, pair of people, not buttocks. Only one thing springs to mind.

Ken Slabby and Gayle O'Toole, *joined together as today's Honorary Worst Persons in the World!*

The Sky Fell

Nominated at the bronze level: Bruce Rheins and Dawn Westlake, who are seeking to trademark and then sell a new wine, complete with a logo that looks half like Christ and half like Michael Jackson, a wine they call "Jesus Juice."

"Jesus Juice" was Jackson's own term for the wine he served his little friends.

The runner-up: The Beijing Lunar Village Aeronautics Science and Technology Company of China, which managed to sell 49 acres of property to 34 customers there, before the authorities came and took them away.

The 49 acres, going for about 37 bucks apiece, were on the Moon, and customers were told that the company represented the "Lunar Embassy" in China.

But the winners . . .

The operators of the AMC Empire 25 Theater on 42nd Street in New York. The crowd of kids in the audience Saturday night were waiting to see the movie *Chicken Little*. Instead, the projectionist showed *Andrea*, a Spanish film that opens with a boy committing suicide.

Mistakes happen, but these folks, say the parents of the traumatized kids, let the wrong film run for five minutes before switching to the *real Chicken Little*.

The AMC Empire 25, *today's Worst Persons in the World!*

Set Up

At the bronze level: Buster the police dog. OK, he's not a person. Sue me. Buster worked for the South Yorkshire Police force in England and was well trained, but shortly after deployment, he began to slack off. In one instance, he was reported to have walked right past a hiding suspect, so he could sidle over to mark his territory. The local constable says Buster has taken early retirement.

Runner-up: Victor Hettigoda, one of the 13 candidates for president of Sri Lanka in next week's election.

You've heard of the campaign promise of "a chicken in every pot"? He's changed it slightly. If he wins, he says, he will use his own funds to give every family in the country its own cow.

And the winner?

Ebony LeMay of Brentwood, Long Island, New York. Her house was broken into Sunday. Two masked men held her and her baby at gunpoint and then pistol-whipped her male friend. So how is she the worst person?

Police say the gunmen were also her friends. She'd arranged to have the guy over at her house so they could rob him. She set up the guy in her own home and used her own baby as a prop.

***Ebony LeMay**, today's Worst Person in the World!*

Wonderbra

NOVEMBER 9, 2005

Nominated at the bronze level: The folks running Shomberg High School in Illinois. Senior Paul Rofus wants to be on the school's bowling team. But Shomberg only has a girls' bowling team. The school is threatening to suspend Rofus, claiming state law prevents him from "playing on a woman's sports team."

The runner-up today: The unnamed suspect in Chicago who attacked 74-year-old Jackie Mlinarcik to get the ring on the pinkie of her left hand. The thief was not subtle. He took her pinkie too.

But the winner . . .

Jill Knispel of Englewood, Florida. She is accused of stealing a newborn green-wing parrot from the pet store at which she works and trading it for a 1964 Volkswagen Karmann Ghia.

How did she smuggle the bird out of the pet shop? She hid it in her brassiere. You know, ma'am, they have introduced the Wonderbra.

***Jill Knispel**, today's Worst Person in the World!*

Who Ya Gonna Call?

NOVEMBER 10, 2005

Nominated at the bronze level: Mayor David Miller of Toronto. City councilors there were surprised to find out that they'd voted themselves a 12 percent pay raise. It was hidden, apparently, in a bill raising salaries for the city's nonunion staff.

Hidden, councilors say, by Mayor Miller.

The runners-up: The voters in the election for the Romoland District School Board near Riverside, California. They have elected Randy Hale. Evidently 831 voters did not wonder why he ran no campaign, made no appearances, didn't even show up at a school board meeting.

See, Board Member–Elect Hale is in prison for a parole violation on previous convictions for spousal abuse and drug possession.

But the winners?

Judge G. Ken Renegar and security guard Wade Gallegos of Urbandale, Iowa. The city of Urbandale had fired Gallegos as a security guard after he reported that the neighborhood he was protecting was haunted by ghosts. Gallegos said that because the city fired him, he deserved unemployment benefits. The city said the hell you do. Judge Renegar has just ruled that Gallegos should get the unemployment insurance!

"This city is headed for a disaster of biblical proportions." Who ya gonna call?

Wade Gallegos and Judge G. Ken Renegar,
today's Worst Persons in the World!

He Had to Carry the
Laundry Upstairs

NOVEMBER 11, 2005

The bronze goes to Megan Oglesbee, a nursing assistant at a nursing home in Westernport, Maryland. She's been convicted of ripping the time-release painkilling patch from the arm of one of the residents and sucking the painkiller out of it.

The runner-up: Gerald Walpin, a member of the Federalist Society. Introducing the governor of Massachusetts at a Society luncheon, he said, "Today when most of the country thinks of who controls Massachusetts, I think the modern day KKK comes to mind. The Kennedy Kerry Klan." The governor, Mitt Romney, has now condemned the introduction.

But at the time, he just laughed.

But the winner?

The one and only Senator Rick Santorum of Pennsylvania. Arguing for a $250,000 cap on malpractice awards, saying "medical lawsuit abuse" is the top health care crisis in his state.

Well, guess who turns out to have testified on behalf of the plaintiff in a malpractice suit against a chiropractor? Yep. When *Mrs.* Rick Santorum sued—for half a million—because of a botched spinal manipulation, the senator testified. He testified that they'd both suffered, she because she gained weight and no longer had the confidence to campaign with him and he because he had to carry the laundry upstairs for her.

Senator Rick Santorum, *today's Worst Person in the World!*

Bald Ego

Bronze winners: The employees of Endemol NV in the Nether-lands. They were setting up dominoes for an attempt at a new world record this week. More than four million of them. Friday night, a sparrow flew in through an open window and knocked over 23,000 dominoes.

That bird paid with his life. An exterminator finally managed to shoot him with an air rifle. But, guys, four million dominos and you leave the window open—and you blame the *bird?!!*

The runner-up: The staff of Saint Mary's Nursing Home in County Monaghan, Ireland, which has found a new way to keep their elderly patients in good cheer: They've added a pub. The patients can booze it up from 11 A.M. to 9 P.M., at regular bar prices. Says assistant director Rose Mooney, "It means the patients aren't bored to death."

No, they drink themselves to death.

But the winner . . .

Alaska governor Frank Murkowski, the man who wanted to charge Bill Clinton for the Ken Starr investigation. He's got another winner: He has had the state upgrade the turbo-prop that previous governors have used and had it buy him a $2.6 million executive jet. An Alaska radio station has called it "Bald-Ego."

Critics say the luxury jet, with its leather furniture and plush carpeting, was an unacceptable waste of taxpayers' money.

Murkowski says the state can afford it and complained that the turbo-prop didn't even have a bathroom. Which led to the runner-up in that name-the-plane radio contest: "Incontinental Airlines."

Governor Frank Murkowski *of Alaska,*
today's Worst Person in the World!

Free for $49.95

At the bronze level: Four street cleaners in Rome. You know that bit where you stand with your back turned to the Fountain of Trevi there? And you throw in a coin? It's supposed to guarantee you'll return to Rome someday.

Where do the coins go? A company retrieves them, splits the money 50–50 with a charity. Not this week. Police say these four street cleaners stole them, as much as 110,000 euros in several weeks.

They say it brings good luck. To those guys.

Runner-up: Brent Bozell, president of the Parents' Television Council. The stats are in: for July of this year, the FCC received 23,547 complaints about indecency on television. Bozell's Parents Television Council says that in July, the number of complaints it filed with the FCC was 23,542. That's right. FCC complaints from the PTC: 23,542. FCC complaints from everybody else in the country: 5.

But the winner . . .

Rush Limbaugh. He is offering the gullible a special patriotic deal. They can "adopt a soldier" and give any U.S. serviceman a "free" subscription to his Web site. All they have to do is pay Rush $49.95. The soldier gets free access to the Web site. And Limbaugh gets nothing out of it, unless you count getting to keep the $49.95!

Rush? I see we've found a new doctor!

You want to donate something to the troops? Just give them free subscriptions! You know: It's called *charity*.

Rush Limbaugh, *today's Worst Person in the World!*

Worse and Worse

NOVEMBER 16, 2005

Bronze winners: The crowd at a Mike Tyson promotional dinner in Darby in England. Police had to be called when a mass brawl broke out. In the crowd, former British champ Frank Bruno, who twice lost in the ring to Tyson. If Bruno landed a punch, it'd be his first ever at any event connected to Cousin Mike.

Runner-up: Well, it could be 37-year-old Lisa Clark of Georgia. She's pregnant. She eloped with the father, married him, and was quickly put in jail. The father is a 15-year-old boy.

But the actual runner-up: Retired Georgia judge Johnny Talent, who married them. You were thinking what exactly, pal?

But the winner . . .

O'Reilly again. This "let Al Qaeda bomb San Francisco" thing just keeps getting worse and worse.

Back on radio he suggested that San Francisco defend itself with a new militia: "You can have a militia that's a rainbow coalition, armed with spatulas . . . and the basic training will be in the Haight. OK, we'll have it right on the Castro Street, march up and down, since they're so good at parades . . ."

So, Bill, now you've insulted all the gay people, too. Tuh-rific.

Do you wonder if he worries about what his job is going to be, in hell?

Bill O'Reilly, *today's Worst Person . . . you know the rest.*

The Low Spark of High-Heeled Boys

NOVEMBER 17, 2005

The bronze: Sharita Williams of Homa, Louisiana. She called 911, summoning police to the Malt-N-Burger in Thibodaux, Louisiana. When they arrived, she explained her complaint and demanded an arrest. The onion rings they served her were cold.

She got the arrest. Police arrested her for misusing 911.

The runner-up: Tasha Henderson of Oklahoma City. The grades of her 14-year-old daughter, Coretha, weren't up to snuff, so Mrs. Henderson made up a sign reading "I don't do my homework and I act up in school, so my parents are preparing me for my future. Will work for food." And she had her daughter stand at an intersection and hold the sign up. The Department of Human Services is investigating.

And psychiatrists are bidding for the future rights to the daughter.

But the winners . . .

The folks who run the Web site of the Republican National Committee. They have assembled a music video of sorts showing Democrats who favored action against Saddam Hussein. It's even appeared on television. No complaint with that. It's the music they've used.

It's the old song by Traffic, "The Low Spark of High Heeled Boys." Jim Capaldi wrote the song with Steve Winwood. Capaldi died earlier this year. Not only was he a pacifist and a vocal critic of the war in Iraq, but his widow today said that the Republican National Committee never even asked for permission to use the song.

The RNC webmasters, *today's Worst Persons in the World!*

Juggling the Facts

NOVEMBER 17, 2005

An Honorary Worst Person in the World: Scooter Libby's attorney, Ted Wells.

The same year we finally found out *who* Deep Throat is, five months later, we were back trying to figure out who is Bob Woodward's *latest* secret source in a White House scandal.

There are many implications to Woodward's belated revelations of his firsthand knowledge of the CIA leak case, but the exculpatory "blockbuster" portrayed by Scooter Libby's attorney Ted Wells is *not* one of them. Wells released a beautiful hunk of "chaff"—the stuff fighter pilots expel to try to throw off enemy radar—in his claim about Woodward's announcement that someone at the White House told *him* about Valerie Plame in June 2003. Wells made it seem as if Woodward had just proved that Libby was *not* the first to leak Plame's name and/or job to a reporter, and that in so doing, Special Prosecutor Patrick Fitzgerald's case had just tumbled to the ground.

But he did it only by altering the truth.

Wells issued a statement at midday, the key passage of which concludes that Woodward's "disclosure shows that Mr. Fitzgerald's statement at his press conference of October 28, 2005, that Mr. Libby was the first government official to tell a reporter about Mr. Wilson's wife was totally inaccurate."

But Fitzgerald didn't say *just* that. The transcript of Fitzgerald's news conference is not disputed—nobody from *his* office has called up trying to get it altered after the fact. On October 28, in his opening statement Fitzgerald *actually* said: "Mr. Libby was the first government official *known* to have told a reporter" about Ambassador Joe Wilson's wife.

That word "known" is a significant qualifier. And although much later, in the question-and-answer portion of his news conference, Fitzgerald described Libby as "at the beginning of the chain of phone calls, the first official to disclose this information outside the government to a reporter," the second statement cannot simply be used in preference to the first. Either the qualifier—expressed virtually at the outset—is considered still in force, or *both* versions ("first official" and "first government official known") have to be included.

Even if the idea that somebody else in the administration might've beaten Libby to the leaking punch *is* relevant to a trial on five counts of lying, the cornerstone of the Wells statement is erroneous—at best, a serious misinterpretation. Fitzgerald was clearly and meticulously leaving his case open in case an earlier leaker later turned up—as evidently he just did. This is no one-word parsing nonsense. Not only does *that* meaning of "known" change entirely the meaning of Fitzgerald's statement, but its related root words (know, knowing, knowingly, etc.) have been the keys to whether or not anybody was indicted for revealing Plame's covert status at the CIA.

The problem, of course, is that such subtlety can shoot right past those who either want to miss it or are in too much of a hurry to check the transcript. I read Wells's quote and thought "That doesn't sound right." The producers of ABC's *World News Tonight* read Wells's quote and evidently didn't hear any such alarm bells. The transcript is not yet out, but at 6:30 EST last night, Elizabeth Vargas stated—and I am paraphrasing—that the Woodward revelations were important because they contradicted Patrick Fitzgerald's statement that Libby *was* the first to leak.

Something deeply symbolic had happened just minutes before ABC's gaffe. Libby and Wells—a former attorney for Philip Morris in the "big tobacco" lawsuits, by the way—emerged from a district courthouse, having spent the afternoon reviewing documents in the case. Wells made a big thing of "thanking" Woodward and asking other reporters to come forward—it's a clever, albeit transparent, spin-job. He and Libby then walked a couple of blocks down the street—*in pouring rain*. Wells couldn't even provide Libby the protection of an umbrella. He is not going to be able to shield him with Woodward's fascinating—but, from the Libby point of view, irrelevant—disclosure.

The question now becomes, of course, who told Woodward and what kind of hay Fitzgerald can make out of that. From among Woodward's statement in the *Washington Post* today, and Jim

VandeHei's first article, and Howard Kurtz's midday follow-up, we have these simple facts in front of us:

- Woodward had conversations with three current or former Bush Administration officials in June 2003 that he thought relevant to Fitzgerald's investigation.

- He identified one of those three—Scooter Libby—in his piece in the *Post* today.

- Woodward said he prepared a list of questions for Vice President Cheney that included a reference to "yellowcake," that he was sending to Libby in June 2003.

- Karl Rove's legal spokesman told the *Post* that Rove wasn't one of the others.

- During the day, Woodward said he'd been authorized by White House Chief of Staff Andy Card to reveal that Card was one of the three White House conversants, but that they did not talk about Plame.

- Don't be misled by the "current or former" Administration figures—the "former" part could easily be a clever sleight-of-hand from Woodward; he provided reams of them in protecting Deep Throat.

The deduction would be that Woodward's source was not Card, Cheney, Libby, or Rove—assuming everybody's telling the truth.

In the interim, for juggling the facts well enough to fool some of the people some of the time . . .

*Ted **Wells**, Scooter Libby's attorney, today's Honorary Worst Person in the World!*

Ham-Burglar

The bronze winner: The European printers of the 100-peso notes for the Phillippines. In the latest batch, they've misspelled the name of the country's president. She's Gloria Arroyo. They spelled it Gloria "Arrovo."

Runner-up: Gilbeto Carnoale of Soverato in southern Italy. He had escaped from house arrest. Chased by local police, he decided to try to hide in the local church, where the other shift of local police were attending mass.

But the winner?

Brian Latuszek, charged with aggravated robbery in Chicago. He was captured after he fell, leaving the bar he had just allegedly robbed. He had stuck the joint up with a "gun-shaped object" that turned out to be a ham sandwich molded into the shape of a gun.

For besmirching the good name of the real Ham-Burglar . . .

Brian Latuszek, *today's Worst Person in the World!*

Unintelligent Designs

The bronze winner: Henry Schmerber, a cement worker on new homes in Eugene, Oregon. He and his colleagues had just finished a house and he celebrated as he always does this time of year by setting up a deep fryer and cooking a turkey. The deep fryer caught fire and burned the brand-new house down.

The runner-up: Mr. Tipsword, first name not known, a 77-year-old hiker who broke his leg in the wilds of Arizona and had to crawl several miles to escape a 250-acre wildfire that broke out in the area. How does that make him one of the worst?

Well, his son says Mr. Tipsword had already broken his leg before the fire. And he'd started a small campfire to get warm. And then he fell into it, scattering the embers and starting the wildfire.

But the winners?

Those fine folks behind the intelligent design nonsense. Because of them, the new exhibition of the work of Charles Darwin at the American Museum of Natural History can't find any corporate sponsors. The corporations are afraid they might tick off the intelligent design guys.

From the same people who brought you "The world is flat" and "The earth is at the center of the universe" and "Let's burn those scientists at the stake" . . .

The folks who dreamt up intelligent design,
today's Worst Persons in the World!

Speaking of Sucking

The bronze winner: William Swanberg of Reno, Nevada. Better known online to you Lego lovers as the proprietor of the Web site Bricklink.com. For three years he's been offering incredible discounts on the plastic building toys. How did he do it? Police say he stole them, $200,000 worth of them, from dozens of Target stores in five western states.

But he's a piker compared to the runners-up: Two custodians at the Casino Korona in the Kranyska Gora Ski Resort in Slovenia. The women clean up the place each night. They're the ones with the giant industrial vacuum cleaners. They've been fired after it turned out they were using the vacuum cleaners to suck the coins out of the slot machines. As much as $566,000 worth.

But the winner . . .

Ann Coulter. Speaking of sucking the coins out of the slot machines. Explaining to her readers—well, reader—that Saddam Hussein was working with Al Qaeda and trying to buy uranium from Niger (because she says so), she has now accused all Democrats of longing "to see U.S. troops shot."

So if you had November 25 as your pick in the pool for the exact day Ann Coulter could no longer be successfully defended at a sanity hearing, you're a winner!

Ann Coulter, *today's Worst Person in the World!*

Ronald MacDonald

NOVEMBER 28, 2005

Nominated at the bronze level: The unnamed fan who ran onto the field yesterday during the Green Bay Packers–Philadelphia Eagles football game and dumped his mother. Well, scattered her ashes. She was a lifelong Eagles fan. No complaint on that point. But consider, this is not like getting your ashes scattered at Yankee Stadium or the Los Angeles Coliseum. The Eagles only opened that stadium two years ago.

The runner-up: The four masked men who held up a struggling business that had just reopened in the Gaza strip. Its zoo. Carrying Kalashnikovs, they stole a lion cub, and two parrots that speak Arabic.

But the winner:

Ronald MacDonald of Manchester, New Hampshire. That's his name. He's 22 years old. He too is accused of theft; in this case, robbery at his place of employment. Where did Ronald MacDonald work?
Wendy's.

Ronald MacDonald, *today's Worst Person in the World!*

Secret Ingredient

NOVEMBER 29, 2005

At the bronze level: The Xcel Energy company in Minnesota. Its customer Daniel Moris had wondered for years why, despite every effort he made to conserve energy, his bill was always so high, nearly 200 bucks a month. Then he happened to notice the number on his electric meter. It wasn't the same as the one on his bill. He's been paying someone else's bill for seven years. The company says it can only adjust Moris's bill for the last three years, so he figures he's out as much as two grand.

The runner-up: Igor Smykov. He's a Russian attorney whose suit has been thrown out in Moscow. So he's going to the European Court of Human Rights in Strasbourg. Who's he suing? *The Simpsons.*
He claims the show has morally damaged his 9-year-old son. *D'oh-s vedanya.*

But the winner . . .

Nancy O'Donnell of Moon, Pennsylvania. Police say the family came over for dinner Saturday night. Her daughter, the kids, the whole group. So she made something special for them. Macaroni and cheese . . . and bleach. Nobody was injured. Ms. O'Donnell faces charges, and possibly a visit to a nice rubber-walled kitchen.

Nancy O'Donnell, *today's Worst Person in the World!*

Triple Crown

The bronze goes to Bill O'Reilly. He's solidified his status as this generation's Joe McCarthy. Just like the Red-Baiter, he now has his own "list." His Web site reads: "The following media operations have regularly helped distribute defamation and false information supplied by far left websites." The list? The *New York Daily News*, the *St. Petersburg Times*, and MSNBC.

You call it "defamation," Bill. We call it precise quotes from your show.

The runner-up: Bill O'Reilly! On *The Today Show* no less—who let *that* happen?—he said, "These pinheads running around going 'get out of Iraq now' don't know what they're talking about. These are the same people before Hitler invaded in World War Two that were saying, 'Ah, he's not such a bad guy.'"

Watch, that'll turn up tomorrow in his list of "defamations."

But the winner . . .

Bill O'Reilly. You know this whole "attack on Christmas" nonsense he made up? Some sort of fantasy in which liberals are coming to your town to force you to not call it Christmas any more? The fantasy that you can't say "Merry Christmas" but only "Happy Holidays"? The thing designed to stir up religious hatred and paranoia in this country? Guess what they're selling over at the Fox News online store? The Fox News Holiday Ornament. And The O'Reilly Factor Holiday Ornament.

Who is trying to change "Merry Christmas" into "Happy Holidays"?

Bill O'Reilly, *that's who, today's Worst Person in the World!*

Where does O'Reilly get this nonsense?

Happy Holidays

DECEMBER 1, 2005

The bronze winners: Howard Fore, the principal of Jasper County Comprehensive School in Monticello, Georgia. An eighth-grade boy discovered a video camera installed in the boys' bathroom. He and some friends removed it to protect their privacy from what they presumed was a pervert somewhere. Nope. It was Principal Fore, who had installed it, he says, to catch anybody vandalizing the bathroom.

He also suspended the student.

Runner-up. Rush Limbaugh. After the kidnapping this week in Iraq of four members of the Christian Peacemaker Teams—including a man from Virginia—the man who keeps the prescription drug industry in business said he wasn't sure the kidnapping wasn't some sort of stunt or fake, and he added, "part of me likes this because I'm eager for people to see reality." Boy, Rush. I hope part of you likes hell . . .

But the winners . . .

Fox News. Again. Remember last night we told you that despite this phony-baloney story they concocted about liberals trying to replace Christmas recognitions with the generic "Happy Holidays," their own Web site was selling "Bill O'Reilly Holiday Ornaments" for your "Holiday tree" instead of "Bill O'Reilly Christmas Ornaments"? Today they changed it. The Web site now identifies the items as "Christmas Ornaments." Hypocritical.

Oh well, at this holiday time of year, let's be forgiving and just be happy in the knowledge that somebody is finally going to hang Bill's "ornaments" from a tree somewhere.

Fox News Channel, *today's Worst Persons in the World!*

Millstone Baseball

DECEMBER 1, 2005

Only the Boston Red Sox could turn the first world championship in 86 years into a court case against one of their own players with the announcement that they have sued former first baseman Doug Mientkiewicz. It was Mientkiewicz who caught the flip from pitcher Keith Foulke to record the final out in the decisive game of the 2004 World Series, that sweep that marked Boston's first win in the fall classic since 1918.

Mientkiewicz kept the ball, and the team's owners later demanded it from him, saying they want to display it as part of the celebration of the end of Boston's incredibly long string of failures. But the value of milestone baseballs having suddenly shot through the roof, $3 million for Mark McGuire's record-breaking home-run ball from 1998, no money-back guarantee, Mientkiewicz said not so fast, that it was his ball and he intended to put his kid through college with it.

But he agreed to lend the ball to the Red Sox for a year while the matter was worked out, saying, I want the fans to see it. The Red Sox then traded Mientkiewicz. Today they sued him, claiming he gained possession of the ball only because he was a Red Sox employee and that the ball is team property.

Of course, precedent is entirely on Mientkiewicz's side. No other team has ever claimed such a baseball from a player. And since the game was played not in the Boston stadium, but rather in the one in St. Louis, if this is going to be decided by the courts, it could very easily be the case that the ball is actually owned not by the Red Sox but by the St. Louis Cardinals.

For tainting a triumph a century in the making . . .

The Boston Red Sox, today's Honorary
Worst Persons in the World!

It's Not the Faith

Bronze winner: Ferrell White. He's the building official for Spring Hill, Tennessee. He has ordered a hair salon to remove "lewd language" from an advertisement in the town. The ad is for products called "Sexy Hair Concepts." The "lewd language," Mr. White says, is the word "sexy."

That's an issue that never arises for our runner-up, Ann Coulter. A two-fer: She posted the personal phone number and e-mail address of a blogger who was critical of her. And she called other groups that disagree with her "Nazi Block Watchers." "You know," she explained, "they tattle on their parents, turn them in to the Nazis."

But the winner, and this one comes with great personal pain because we were friends when he worked here, and thereafter . . .

John Gibson. Selling his new book about this phony-baloney "war on Christmas," John revealed an ugly side to himself. He's one of those people who think all religions but his are mistaken. You know, the way a lot of religious nutbag terrorists think.

"I would think," Gibby said on a syndicated radio show, "if somebody is going to be—have to answer for—following the wrong religion, they're not going to have to answer to me. We know who they're going to have to answer to."

I'd tell you which religion John thinks is the only one that's right, but what's the difference. It's not the faith that's the issue. It's the intolerance.

John Gibson, *today's Worst Person in the World!*

The Lice-Man Cometh

Bronze winner: Bill O'Reilly. Apparently you have him to thank for the recent minor drop in gas prices. He told an interviewer: "I have guys inside the five major oil companies . . . they got scared because of my reporting and reporting of some others. They said, 'uh ho.'" Thanks, Bill.

You know, there are more potholes than usual this winter in New York City. Could you get them filled? Feel free to use your contacts, or your superior mind, or whatever.

Runner-up: The Ford Motor Company. It has long been a supporter of gay rights causes, advertising its products in gay media, etc. Friday it announced it was canceling its ad campaigns for Jaguar and Land Rover in such publications, this after months of boycotting by a bunch of homophobes called the American Family Association. Nice. Folding up faster than the bumper on a Festiva.

But the winner . . .

Dr. Dale Pearlman of Menlo Park, California. He has been selling an experimental, revolutionary anti-lice lotion. You know, for kids. "Dry-on suffocation-based pediculocide." Cost: $285, which includes the cost of a doctor's visit.

He has now admitted that it's actually just a bottle of Cetaphil Cleanser in a different package. Wholesale cost: $10. And now available without a prescription.

The Lice-Man Cometh . . .

Dr. Dale Pearlman, *today's Worst Person in the World!*

DCPD Blues

There's a theme to these.

The bronze goes to the manager at a Citgo station in Gary, Indiana. Rosetta Heffner was robbed at knifepoint while filling up the church van. She ran to the clerk for help, asked him to call the cops. He replied, "Use your cell phone." The manager says the clerks are instructed not to call the cops because the criminals will get mad at them.

Runner-up: Motorists, maybe police, anybody with a car who spent a weekend driving past the lump at the side of the road near Franklin, Pennsylvania. Sure, it was tan and slightly covered with snow, but it wasn't a deer carcass. It was a pedestrian who had been run over by a car. And left to lie there for three days.

But the winner . . .

An unidentified Washington, D.C., police officer. Charles Atherton, the urban designer, former secretary of the U.S. Commission on Fine Arts, was hit by a car in the capital over the weekend. As he lay there, unresponsive, badly injured, witnesses saw the cop come over and give him a ticket for jaywalking. Mr. Atherton died shortly thereafter.

For not thinking the old man lying in the street might've needed something more than a $5 jaywalking citation . . .

A Washington, D.C., police officer, *today's*
Worst Person in the World!

None More Blak

Bronze winner: Derrick Ford of Port Jervis, New York, under arrest after trying to win a $10 bet. A pal wagered he couldn't bite the head off a gecko. He could. Mr. Ford evidently didn't know it was animal cruelty, and apparently he forgot he was on probation.

The runner-up: A former employer at the Harbor Island fuel depot in Washington state, suspected of doing what many ex-employees in many lines of business have done: left with a little of the merchandise. In his case, some gasoline.

A million dollars' worth.

But the winners . . .

The Coca-Cola Company. It is introducing a new cola called "Blak," first in France, and later here. It describes the soda as having the "true essence of coffee, a rich smooth texture, and a coffee-like froth when poured." You got it. Coke is going to start selling carbonated cold coffee.

The Coca-Cola Company, *today's Worst Persons in the World!*

The Horror, the Horror

Bronze winners: The Florida Marlins baseball team. Some season ticket holders are asking for refunds after the Marlins traded away their catcher, their first baseman, their second baseman, their third baseman, their centerfielder, and one of their starting pitchers after raising ticket prices. Today the Marlins not only said no, but the team issued a snippy statement saying they "continue to deliver to season ticket holders exactly what was promised to them: exciting and talented Major League Baseball players."

True, except they're all on the *visiting* team.

Runner-up: Bill O'Reilly. Here we go again. Proudly reminded his audience that he "didn't put Abu Ghraib pictures on this broadcast, the only television journalist not to do so." Wait, wait—you think you're a television journalist?

But the winner . . .

Yes! Him again! On radio, getting hysterical about this anti-Christmas nonsense, he said he would get the "anti-Christian forces in this country" who are trying to "diminish and denigrate the holiday." Here's the good part: "I'm going to use all the power that I have on radio and television to bring horror into the world of people who are trying to do that."

"Bring horror," he said.

Bill, just remember, to "bring horror" into this world, all you have to do is open your mouth.

Bill O'Reilly, *today's Worst Person in the World!*

Queso No Fresco

DECEMBER 9, 2005

The bronze goes to the Cartoon Network. No, not the fine folks who bring you the reruns of *Family Guy* and *The Boondocks* and all that. This is the ring of marijuana dealers in New York City who call themselves "the Cartoon Network" and whom DEA officers busted up this week, mentioning in passing that they not only sold pot to thousands of customers, they delivered it.

Runner-up: The police who work for the Dallas rapid transit service. According to witnesses quoted by the newspaper the *Dallas Observer*, late last month they arrested a man named Todd Lyon for jaywalking across the railroad tracks. Problem is, the witnesses say he wasn't jaywalking, and the cops hit him and his 14-year-old son, and cuffed him, and took him to jail, where he languished for 11 days because he couldn't make bail, before he pleaded out just to go home.

But the winner . . .

Jessica Sandy Booth, an 18-year-old woman under arrest in Memphis. She spotted a brick of cocaine in a home she was visiting. She decided she wanted it, so she allegedly hired a hit man to help her break in, kill the four residents, and steal the cocaine.

Bad news for her, part one: the hit man was an undercover cop.

Bad news for her, part two: the "brick of cocaine" she saw was actually a block of queso fresco Mexican cheese.

Jessica Sandy Booth, *today's Worst Person in the World!*

The Balloon

DECEMBER 12, 2005

Bronze winner: Kirstie Adams of Uttoxeter in England. Remember that St. Louis Cardinals' fan and how it was included in her obituary that she was happy that the team had just traded away a pitcher she didn't like? Mrs. Adams is the mirror image. She gave birth to a boy, and 25 minutes later she registered him as a member of the fan club of the British soccer team Darby County.

Twenty-five minutes later.

The runner-up: Joe L. Light of Memphis, Tennessee. For decades we've heard about people like Mr. Light, but this is the first time somebody like him has been identified. It turns out he voted in the special Tennessee State Senate election on September 15, which is a neat trick, given that Mr. Light died on August 6.

But the winner . . .

Warren Roberts, owner of a strip club in Birmingham, England. He says he and a local hot-air balloon operator have combined forces, and, when it gets warm, they will launch a balloon 150 feet in the air, on which customers will be able to get lap dances.

Hey listen, if the customers could get it to go up 150 feet in the air, they wouldn't need lap dances.

What? The Balloon. Get the *balloon* to go up. What did you think I meant?

Warren Roberts, *today's Worst Person in the World!*

Plano Truth

The bronze: An unnamed couple from Luton, in England. They decided to have a romp in the bathroom of a 777 flying to Jamaica. They were so noisy that the flight crew ordered them back to their seats. They were so drunk that they started spitting at the flight attendants. They were so threatening that the plastic handcuffs were not sufficient to restrain them. The plane had to make an emergency landing in Bermuda. British Airways says it is billing the couple for said landing.

$3.8 million.

Runner-up: Wally O'Dell, the chairman and CEO of Diebold, the company that makes automatic teller machines and little computerized voting gizmos that leave no record. Mr. O'Dell is the man who, as part of the Republican campaign in Ohio, infamously declared he would "deliver" that state to Mr. Bush last year, then agreed his remarks were inappropriate. He's resigned for personal reasons, although those personal reasons might be financial in nature; we're waiting for that story to break.

But the winner . . .

Yeah, him again.

You know how we've been telling you he's been making up this blarney about a plot against Christmas? Well, I had meant the term "making up" metaphorically. Silly me.

O'Reilly told his TV audience that a school in Plano, Texas, was so anti-Christmas that it had told its kids not to wear red and green during the holidays. And he told his radio audience that the entire township of Saginaw, Michigan, had done the same thing. Plano's superintendent of schools had to contact parents to tell them O'Reilly was wrong. Saginaw's township manager Ron Lee, wearing a red shirt and a Santa Claus tie and sitting next to a Christmas tree, has demanded a retraction.

Where does O'Reilly get this nonsense? Oh, take a guess. Once again . . .

Bill O'Reilly, *today's Worst Person in the World!*

Come On, Pretty Mama

DECEMBER 14, 2005

The bronze: To the aides to Senate Majority Leader Bill Frist. Unhappy with questions put to their boss by a reporter from the Associated Press about those dubious family stock sales, the aides verbally attacked the reporter—in front of about three dozen other reporters. As the old saw goes: never get into a fight with people who buy ink by the barrel.

The runner-up: Neal Boortz, who is another one of these radio commentators who gives free speech a bad name. In a blog post, Boortz predicted that California governor Arnold Schwarzenegger would commute the sentence of convicted killer Stanley "Tookie" Williams because, if he didn't, "there will be riots in South Central Los Angeles and elsewhere." Boortz added, "There are a lot of aspiring rappers and NBA superstars who could really use a nice flat-screen television right now."

So the guy's not only got no handle on predicting events, but he's also a racist?

But the winner . . .

Tiffany Eagle of Kokomo, Indiana. She and her girlfriend Ashley Tomaszewski decided to go drinking at 3 A.M. this past Sunday at a strip club there. We have no complaint with that. When police asked Ms. Eagle where her 3-month-old son happened to be, she said she'd left him with the sitter. Why, then, they asked, is the baby out in the backseat of your unheated car?

Despite outdoor temperatures of 32 degrees, the baby was fine. Mom went to the big house on charges of felony neglect and public intoxication.

Tiffany Eagle, *today's Worst Person in the World!*

False Arrest

DECEMBER 14, 2005

A man accused of stalking and harassing a CNN anchor has sued her and her husband for a million dollars.

Lincoln Kareem had been angry over an effort to remove a hawk's nest from the Manhattan building where Paula Zahn lives. Her husband, Richard Cohen, had led the effort to remove the nest.

A year ago, Mr. Kareen was arrested on charges of stalking, harassment, and child endangerment for having screamed at Zahn and her husband and 7-year-old son, "House of shame, bring back the nest."

Although the charges against him were later dropped, he has now sued them, claiming they caused his "false arrest."

For not quitting while he was ahead . . .

Lincoln Kareem, today's Honorary Worst Person in the World!

Catholics Against Christmas

The bronze winner: Quentin Wilson, an employee at a Waffle House in Stockbridge, Georgia. Police accuse him of offering a homeless man who was camped out near the restaurant five dollars to drink a cocktail. The cocktail consisted of a chemical cleaning solution—it ate through the victim's esophagus, tongue, and gums and left him on a ventilator. So far all they've got on Wilson is a charge of misdemeanor reckless conduct, but they may go for a felony.

The runner-up: Wal-Mart again, this time the one at the Islandia Shopping Center in Central Islip, New York. The local high school choir had just finished a church performance when it went across the street and started doing impromptu caroling at the mall. All the stores, including the Stop & Shop, welcomed the singers with open arms. The managers at Wal-Mart called the cops.

And the winner . . .

I know, I know, we're going to ban him soon, but the material he produces—we couldn't buy this stuff.

The latest part of his delusion about a war on Christmas? That it's partially the fault of the Catholic Church. Now this is a tough sell. The prelates and the cardinals and the archbishops aren't "standing up for Christmas," he says. "They were MIA in the priest/pedophilia scandals. Now they're MIA in the Christmas Controversy."

Catholics against Christmas. You know what's MIA, Bill? Your brain.

Once again . . .

Bill O'Reilly, *today's Worst Person in the World!*

Man of Stone

DECEMBER 27, 2005

The bronze goes to Santa Claus. Well, not *the* Santa Claus. People who usurped his identity, like the idiots who trotted a guy in the suit out on TV and insisted Santa is a Republican. And the security people at a Jakarta hotel who dressed up as Santa as they used metal detectors to look for car bombs over the weekend, and no doubt traumatize any 6-year-olds in the neighborhood.

The runner-up: Mr. Jesus Christ. No, not *the* Mr. Jesus Christ. This is the former Mr. Jose Luis Espinal of New York City, whose petition to legally change his name to Jesus Christ was granted by a judge. The judge says the state can deny an application only if somebody with the same name objects.

But the winner . . .

Stalin! The dead dictator of the Soviet Union. You've gotta be pretty worst to win the honors 52 years after you die, yet there you have it. The newspaper *The Scotsman* revealed the discovery of Stalin's secret plans dating to the 1920s to create a new stalwart fighting man for the Red Army. "Insensitive to pain, resistant, and indifferent about the quality of food they eat," they quote him as saying. No, he wasn't proposing to draft Englishmen into the Soviet Military.

Stalin wanted to breed through artificial insemination a cross between humans—and chimpanzees. Which explains this guy!

Ioseph Vissarionovich Dzhugashvili, *a.k.a. Stalin, today's Worst Person in the World!*

Bring Your Own Shovel

DECEMBER 28, 2005

The bronze winner: Tricia Owens of Edison, Ohio. Arrested and charged with robbing a bank in Mount Gilead, she explained that she'd gotten the idea from her brother when he robbed the same bank four years ago. She even wore a wire to record him admitting he'd done it. Thanks, Sis.

The runner-up: Reno Tobler, a truck driver from Clive, Iowa. Police picked him up for hurling detergent-sized bottles into the backyards of houses he passed. Inside the bottles? His own urine.

Yes, it's really bad, but look at the bright side: at least he left it in the bottles.

But the winner . . .

Lisa Carlson of St. George, Vermont, one of the backers of a plan there to take 50 acres of undeveloped public land and turn it into a garden park, nature reserve, and do-it-yourself cemetery.

That's right: families could go dig their own graves, for their own loved ones. No fuss, no muss, no caskets, no embalming. Just bring your own shovels, and fill 'er up. As the character Lou Grant said on the "Chuckles" episode of *The Mary Tyler Moore Show*: "I don't want anybody to make any fuss. When I go, I just want to be stood outside in the garbage with my hat on."

Lisa Carlson, *today's Worst Person in the World!*

My Three Sons

Bronze winners: Donovan Blackburn, city manager of Pikeville, Kentucky. How to improve economic conditions there, he wonders. Aha, he concludes, talk a coal company into mining, and then knocking down, two of the mountaintops that surround the town. More money, more room for houses, and of course more chance of ecological disaster.

The runner-up: Juan Reyes, a 37-year-old man babysitting two toddlers in Patchogue, on Long Island, New York. Mr. Reyes was discovered, passed out and drunk, and the 2-year-old child was having more trouble standing than usual, and his breath smelled of alcohol. Mr. Reyes has been arrested.

But the winner . . .

Police officer Jared Ginglen of Chicago and his two brothers. They were looking at pictures of a bank robbery taken by surveillance cameras when one of them looked at the silver-plated gun the robber was holding and said, "Isn't that the gun we gave Dad last year?" Another looked at the robber and said, "And isn't that Dad holding it?"

The Ginglens promptly gave up their 64-year-old father to the authorities.

William Ginglen was sentenced today to 40 years in jail after he was turned in by My Three Sons.

Jared Ginglen and his two brothers, *today's Worst Persons in the World!*

He walked right into a propeller again.

Je Ne Sais Quoi

JANUARY 2, 2006

The bronze winner: Sabina Nakajima, violinist of San Francisco. She had borrowed a $175,000, 300-year-old violin from a music shop "on spec." If she liked it, she'd buy it. She put it in the trunk of her car, she said, then the car was towed. When she got it back, the violin was missing. She even gave somber TV interviews to that effect. Police have announced that Ms. Nakajima has now recanted her story that the violin was stolen. You can figure out the rest.

Number two: Manufacturers of the talking book *Potty Time with Elmo*. As one Dallas mother found out, somebody decided to screw around with at least some of a recent press run. The book is supposed to say, in Elmo's voice, "Who wants to try to go potty?" In this book, it instead says, "Who wants to die?"

But the winners—kind of a theme here—

The processors and consumers of the most expensive coffee in the world, Kopi Luwak, from Indonesia. $175 a pound. Why so expensive? Because the beans are first eaten by a nocturnal jungle animal called the palm civet, then passed through its digestive tract, adding a certain *je ne sais quoi* to the flavor.

Hey, why does this stuff cost $175 a pound if they've literally got it coming out of their backsides?

The processors and consumers of Kopi Luwak coffee, *today's Worst Persons in the World!*

Soccer's First Rule

JANUARY 3, 2006

Maybe we can just *permanently* bronze him. The latest: A flat-out threat against columnist Frank Rich and editor Bill Keller of the *New York Times*. He says the *Times* has been "unfair in its coverage of the Bush White House," so "if they want to attack people personally then we're going to have to just show everybody about their lives."

Bill, nobody cares about their lives. If people cared about the personal lives of people in newspaper or television, you'd be working the change booth at a video arcade.

The silver: A former employee at a Honolulu Wal-Mart, believed to be responsible for tampering. Rachel Cambra bought an iPod at the store for her 14-year-old daughter. And instead found inside the box a hunk of raw meat. Lady, you want fries with that iPod?

But the winner . . .

The Crowne Plaza Hotel at the airport in Orlando. Its managers booked two events over the weekend. The hotel hosted the Clearwater Chargers and other soccer teams made up of boys 13 and under, some from Catholic schools. And it also hosted 200 members of a local swingers association. A middle-aged swingers association.

Parents say they had to explain to the kids why the swingers were dancing naked or kept changing partners. Presumably they also had to remind them of soccer's first rule: Don't touch anything with your hands.

***The managers of the Crowne Plaza Airport Hotel in Orlando**, today's Worst Persons in the World!*

Disturbing and Disgraceful

JANUARY 4, 2006

The context of the 1972 Olympic massacre could not have been more different than that of the Sago Mine disaster, or the initial reporting about it. But the structures of the two stories have striking similarities.

Unfortunately, there was not one Jim McKay in West Virginia, although some, such as MSNBC's Robert Hager, counseled caution as time wore on, after the initial reports of rescue without any official word from West Virginia's governor.

The Associated Press, though, had bulletined that news at 11:52 P.M. on January 3, reporting, "Twelve miners caught in an explosion in a coal mine were found alive Tuesday night, more than 41 hours after the blast, family members said."

That the family members said it, and it was often broadcast as fact, may be just one of the issues here, but broadcast coverage mirrored the AP report: "Bells at a church where relatives had been gathering rang out as family members ran out screaming in jubilation."

Every major and practically every other newspaper followed suit as editors faced the first-edition deadlines of their East Coast publications. Some papers put the qualifier in the headline. The *New York Times* declared: "Twelve Miners Found Alive, Family Members Say." The *Times* was also one of the publications that cited official sources as well as family members—official sources who ultimately were wrong.

Based on what the coal company is now saying was a garbled message from the rescue workers themselves still in the mine to the central command, the families were told the 12 miners were alive. Naturally, they celebrated and gave thanks and told reporters.

But the company discovered within 30 minutes that the good news was just an illusion. Yet by their own account, they waited more than two hours to tell the families. The old joke about a lie getting halfway around the world while the truth is still getting its pants on has never been more tragically illustrated.

"One of the most disturbing and disgraceful media performances of its kind in recent years," wrote the editor of *Editor and Publisher* magazine, Greg Mitchell, today.

For putting sensation before substance . . .

The mainstream media, today's Honorary Worst Persons in the World!

Man of God

There's Mr. and Mrs. Jacob Calero of San Roman, California. Police say they went to Las Vegas for five days of New Year's fun. They left their brand new puppies with a dog-sitter, but their 5- and 10-year-old sons? They let them stay in their house—home alone.

The silver? Pastor Lonnie Latham of the South Tulsa Baptist Church, an executive committee member of the Southern Baptist Convention, who has encouraged his flock to try to convert gays and lesbians from their "sinful, destructive lifestyle." Pastor Latham's been arrested, charged with propositioning an undercover police officer who he thought was a male prostitute. Oopsie.

But the winner, a more prominent "Man of God" . . .

Pat Robertson. He told his TV audience today that Ariel Sharon's stroke happened because God was angry at the Israeli prime minister for proposing to "carve up and give away" God's land. Uh-huh.

You ever get the feeling that if there's an afterlife, Pat Robertson's going to spend his first thousand years in it really, *really* surprised?

Pat Robertson, *today's Worst Person in the World!*

Pity His Listeners

At the bronze level: Nadine Nunnelee, a teacher at Garden City High School in Kansas. Our friends at TheSmokingGun.com reported she is the ceremonial first teacher arrested in the new year for sleeping with one of her underage students.

The runner-up: Judge Edward Cashman in Burlington, Vermont, and the state corrections department there. Finding Mark Hulett guilty of repeatedly sexually assaulting a girl over a period of four years starting when she was 6, the department recommended and he agreed that Hulett is a "low risk for committing a similar crime," so he's been sentenced to 60 days in jail.

Days.

But the winner . . .

The indescribable Rush Limbaugh. He has now defended the president bypassing the Foreign Intelligence Surveillance Courts to authorize those NSA wiretaps by explaining to his audience that it was one of those FISA court judges who "wouldn't let" the FBI examine the laptop of the so-called 20th hijacker, Zacarias Moussaoui, and thus perhaps discover the 9/11 plot in the summer of 2001.

In fact, the FBI never even went to court; never even asked a judge to let it read Moussaoui's computer. The FBI's own lawyers decided the bureau didn't have the right to examine the computer. A later investigation suggested that those FBI lawyers were wrong and if they'd only gone to one of the FISA judges, the judge would've granted access to Moussaoui's computer. But of course that's not the kind of story that Limbaugh wants you to know.

So he lied about it and told it backward. Which is why his listeners live in ignorance.

And why, once again, . . .

Rush Limbaugh *is today's Worst Person in the World!*

Think Twice

The bronze, fittingly enough, to U.S. Olympic skier Bode Miller, who has revealed that he has often skied drunk, even in competition, that there are no rules against it, and that he may do it again.

Our runner-up: Gayle Ruzicka, president of the Utah Eagle Forum. Cheering the news that a theater in Sandy, Utah, had cancelled, at the last moment, the opening of the gay cowboy movie, *Brokeback Mountain*, Ms. Ruzicka told reporters that the cave-in "tells the young people especially that maybe there is something wrong with this show."

Or, ma'am, it tells them that maybe there's something wrong with the Utah Eagle Forum, and bigotry.

But the winner . . .

Brian Lewis, a press flak at FNC. He responded to the fact that we called out his company on its latest set of on-air news atrocities by telling the Associated Press, "Perhaps Jeff Zucker should think twice about tying his future, not to mention the reputation of General Electric, to an unstable ratings-killer like Keith, who uses an NBC property for his personal attacks."

There's lots of ways I could go here, but since they use ratings the way rich people use money, how are those ratings doing for:

Geraldo Rivera At Large
Nanny 9-1-1
Arrested Development
Stacked
Fox Sports Net
Bones
Andy Richter Controls the Universe
Titus
Wanda At Large
A Minute with Stan Hooper
Cedric the Entertainer
Pasadena

Keen Eddy
That 80's Show
Normal, Ohio
The Tick
Cracking Up
The War at Home
Popeye's Voyage
Fox and Friends First
Bill O'Reilly's viewers under the age of 90.

OK. Well, that's about half the list . . .

Brian Lewis, *today's Worst Person in the World!*

Errors

JANUARY 10, 2006

For nearly 70 years now, sportswriters have been doing most of the electing of the members of baseball's Hall of Fame. And for nearly all that time, they have been screwing it up.

They corrected one error this day but left another two or three dozen unaddressed, as usual. Bruce Sutter, the brilliant relief pitcher of the Cubs, Cardinals, and Braves, finally got enough votes to get elected this afternoon by the 520 voters from the Baseball Writers Association of America. Sutter shares the all-time record for leading a league in saves. He did it five times.

But it took until this, his thirteenth time on the ballot, for the writers to elect him. They still managed to bypass his contemporary in bullpen acedom, the legendary Goose Gossage, terrifying fireballer of the Yankees and White Sox and Padres and others. He finished third in the voting this year, behind the Red Sox star slugger Jim Rice, whom the voters have been insulting annually since 1995, even though during the era in which he played, he led all his contemporaries in runs batted in and total bases and was second in homers and second in batting average. The writers also again ignored Dale Murphy. From 1978 through 1991 he hit more home runs than anybody else in baseball, but he ended his career with 398 homers instead of the nice round 400, which apparently has confused the writers ever since.

This was a player so exemplary that after winning the most valuable player award in 1982, he was still unhappy about a late-season batting slump, so he spent the first few weeks of the off-season with the Braves minor leaguers down in the Florida fall instructional league. Murphy got only 56 votes.

Ignored in the voting process is the fact that most baseball writers regularly see only the team that they cover. Their familiarity with players from other teams or the other league might be less than that of a good fan. It is noted that of the 520 ballots the writers returned this year in the vote, 12 were blank. It's assumed that that was some sort of protest there. But given their track record, there is an excellent chance that those 12 writers simply didn't know how to fill those ballots out.

***The members of the Baseball Writers Association of America**, today's Honorary Worst Persons in the World!*

Two's a Crowd

The bronze: C'mon, Bill, you can do better than this.

As part of his latest debate (with reality), the Big Giant Head has gone on the radio to protest UNICEF spokesman Harry Belafonte by saying, "If Josef Stalin was still alive, he'd be the UNICEF spokesman." Bill, are you remembering to wear a helmet when you go outside, so when you finally fall over you don't break anything? I'm concerned.

Our runner-up: Pat Robertson. He's trying to soften the impact of his remarks last week, equating the stroke suffered by Israeli prime minister Ariel Sharon with biblical vengeance against those who tried to divide God's land.

Is he doing this out of remorse? Not exactly. He's trying to mollify the Israeli tourist ministry, with whom he and a bunch of evangelicals had been negotiating to build a Bible theme park in Galilee. The Israelis had said they wouldn't deal with him after the line about Sharon. So Pat may get those mystical visions, but he apparently can still see the money.

But the winner . . .

Idaho state senate president Robert Geddes. Seeing the prison population overcrowding problem in Idaho, he has asked, "Why does every inmate need his or her own bed?" He is suggesting they sleep in shifts. Apart from the problem noted by the state's corrections director, that this would mean doubling the population of each prison . . . hmmm . . . putting prisoners two to a bed.

Evidently Senator Geddes has never seen the HBO series *Oz*.

*Idaho state senate president **Robert Geddes**,*
today's Worst Person in the World!

Practically Imperfect in Every Way

JANUARY 12, 2006

The bronze: Tracy L. Mayfield of Jackson, Missouri. Police went to her house because her dog was making too much noise. They say she threatened them with a knife and a stun gun. Then started taking off her clothes. And, finally, threatened them with a sex toy.

Police say they found pipes for crystal meth and pot, also klonopin and librax. And the walls of the house were melting.

The runner-up: Kathleen Rice, the newly elected district attorney of Nassau County, New York. She has hired as her executive assistant, at a salary of $95,000 a year, a woman named Cheryl Rice. They happen to be sisters-in-law. So?

Kathleen Rice's campaign platform? Merit-based hiring.

But the winners . . .

Jany Chumas of Eau Claire, Wisconsin, and the unidentified contractors who refinished the drywall in a room in her house earlier this month.

None of them apparently had the common sense to remove Ms. Chumas's cat from the house before beginning work. Several days after the wall was closed up, Ms. Chumas began to hear faint mewing sounds from the construction area. They finally punched a hole in the wall and her cat, Mary Poppins, came staggering out from where she'd been trapped for five days.

Jany Chumas and her drywall folks, *today's*
Worst Persons in the World!

Allegedly the Worst

The bronze goes to Karen Durante, a postal carrier in Lyons, Colorado. If you live there, and you ordered some of those movies-by-mail DVDs, you've probably been wondering why you didn't get them. Police charge that Ms. Durante stole a few of them. According to court documents, 503 were missing.

The runner-up: Houston district fire chief Jack Williams and the civil service regulations he upheld, which resulted in firefighter Beda Kent having to take a promotion exam at 9 A.M. Wednesday—just twelve hours after she gave birth to a daughter.

But the winner . . .

Brent Bozell. His Cybercast News Service is apparently trying to start another one of those "Swift Boat Veterans" hatchet jobs, this time against Vietnam vet Congressman Jack Murtha of Pennsylvania just as Murtha is predicting that the "vast majority of U.S. troops will be out of Iraq by the end of the year."

The CNS News story is a rehash of 25 years of unproven allegations that Murtha, who volunteered to go to Vietnam and won two Purple Hearts there, didn't deserve them. In massaging those charges, Bozell's writers use the following words: allege, alleging, apparently, appears, indicated, may, and reportedly.

Brent Bozell, *today's Worst Person in the World!*

Game Misconduct

The bronze to whoever runs the jury-duty computer in New Bedford, Massachusetts. It has summoned Kaylee Reynolds to serve. Kaylee is 2 years old. The explanation: a local census form was screwed up, and Kaylee's birth date was entered as "July 4th, 1776." Well, that makes her 229 years old. You wanted a 229-year-old to serve on the jury?

The runner-up: Kelly Houston, affirmative action officer of Greenwich, Connecticut. Accused by the wives of former New York Mets players Bobby Bonilla and Sheila Foster with discrimination after they were denied admittance to an exercise class at a beach there last June.

Ms. Houston said it wasn't discrimination. It was that Mrs. Bonilla and Mrs. Foster didn't have the residency cards required to use the Greenwich beach. Then, according to the *Hartford Courant*, somebody discovered the e-mail Ms. Houston had sent three weeks earlier to organizers of the exercise class suggesting he cut the number of black participants in his class.

Oops.

But the winner . . .

The assistant referee in a Swedish Hockey League game between Sveg IK and Halsingegardens AIK. Players on both teams couldn't figure out what his hand signals meant. Then he started dropping his whistle. Finally a few of them skated close to him and noticed the smell on his breath. He was drunk. They sent him home after the second period. Well, a similar story would explain what those football referees were doing over the weekend.

The assistant ref in the Swedish Hockey League,
today's Worst Person in the World!

Conversational, Not Confrontational

The bronze: Michael Acosta. As a Chicago police commander, he handled $9,000 worth of contributions to a ceremony to honor heroic officers in that city. And today he admitted he kept $4,000 of it.

The silver: Dr. Mojgan Azari of London, England. You've heard George Carlin's joke about how, statistically, there has to be a worst doctor in the world?

She's a dentist. Her boyfriend is not. That didn't stop her from letting him fill in for her on at least 600 patients, according to police. He drilled cavities and put in fillings without anesthetic and without knowing what he was doing.

But the winner . . .

Ken Jautz, the president of CNN Headline News. Today he hired talk-show yakker Glenn Beck to host his own prime-time show. Jautz called Beck "cordial," saying his show was "conversational, not confrontational." I guess that's why last September, Beck said, of all the Hurricane Katrina survivors in New Orleans, "The only ones we're seeing on television are the scumbags. It is exactly like the 9/11 victims' families. There's about 10 of them that are spoiling it for everybody."

That's cordial? Compared to *who*? Bill O'Reilly? Michael Savage?

Ken Jautz, *today's Worst Person in the World!*

Martin Luther Bill

JANUARY 18, 2006

The bronze: To whoever it was who flung the rock through the living room window at the California home of NFL referee Pete Morelli. Morelli was the man who erroneously overturned a Pittsburgh Steelers' interception in Sunday's playoff game against Indianapolis. Police are presumably looking for somebody incredibly stupid, because while his mistaken call gave Indianapolis some points in that game, Pittsburgh still won it.

The runner-up: Andrew Jones, founder of a radical group of UCLA graduates called the Bruin Alumni Association. Jones is offering students up to a hundred bucks per class to supply tapes or notes "exposing" any UCLA professor who expresses left-wing political views.

Mr. Jones claims he graduated from the university in 2003, although you have to wonder how, if he felt his own beliefs or views were so weak that they might be mysteriously transformed or altered by a professor.

But our winner . . .

Oh, dear. What now? Nothing to do with Martin Luther King Day, I hope. Oops. There he goes.

"I don't think Dr. King would be disappointed in where the economic situation is in the U.S.A. right now," he said on the radio.

So? That sounds passable. Wait? There was more?

Ohhhhhh: "I'm the poster boy for that. And, you know, no matter what color you are, if you work hard, and you're persistent, and you get educated, you can make it here."

Economic opportunity. On Martin Luther King Day. You're the poster boy. Bill?

You know you're . . . I mean, I hate to break this to you, but . . . you do know . . . you're *white*.

Bill O'Reilly, *today's Worst Person in the World!*

Savage Reminder

The bronze: To Andrei Kornilov, elephant trainer of Russia's "Around the World Circus." They're having a really cold winter there—22 below, at times. So to keep them warm, Mr. Kornilov is giving his elephants buckets of vodka.

Apart from the medical implications here, one of the elephants responded by swinging his trunk wildly and promptly breaking the circus's only heater.

The silver: The school board at McHenry Community High School in Illinois. It has expelled 16-year-old Derek Kelly for drawing gang signs. Of course, what he drew was a crown, a cross, and a spiderweb, and his initials, "D.L.K." The school board assumes this had something to do with either the Latin Kings gang or the Latin Disciples gang. Even though Derek is not a gang member and, oh, by the way, the drawing he did was in his own notebook.

But the winner . . .

Glenn Beck, the radio talk-show host to whom CNN just gave a show on Headline News, calling him "conversational, not confrontational."

On the radio he had a mock contest to see which public figure was the "biggest prostitute." Among the selections: Cindy Sheehan. Beck said, "That's a pretty big prostitute there." Then his producer corrected him and said Sheehan should be called a "tragedy pimp."

Let me say to my friends at CNN, who gave me my first break in TV:

Hey, guys. About this Glenn Beck show. From personal experience, maybe you should bail on this, right now. Two simple words: Michael. Savage.

Glenn Beck, *today's Worst Person in the World!*

Fan Interference

JANUARY 19, 2006

It might seem like a pro athlete goes into the stands to confront a fan about once a week, but it is clearly not every day when the athlete in question headed for the seats because he thought his own wife was in danger, or when that athlete happens to be the president of the National Basketball Association Player's Union. Or when the fan says he's going to sue that player for $1 million.

The crowd at last night's Knicks/Bulls game in Chicago was 21,268—21,269 if you count Antonio Davis of the Knicks. During overtime Davis suddenly dashed over the scorers' table and raced to where his wife, Kendra, was sitting. His coach, Larry Brown, said Davis thought he saw his wife falling back, although there's no evidence that there was any physical confrontation between Kendra Davis and an unidentified Chicago fan. For his part, Antonio Davis never raised his hands and left the scene as arena security arrived. All he has said thus far is, "I witnessed my wife being threatened by a man that I learned later to be intoxicated. I saw him touch her and I know I should not have acted the way I did, but I would have felt terrible if I didn't react. There was no time to call security, it happened too quickly."

But the fan has now identified himself and said that Davis's description of him is "A lie." Twenty-two-year-old Michael Axelrod said he was not drunk, he was just booing a call at Davis's team, when Kendra Davis came up and put both her hands on his face and tried to scratch him. Axelrod said he never touched Mrs. Davis and that he called security. "I was glad she was done hitting me," Axelrod added, "but I didn't want her to hit anybody else."

Other fans say Mrs. Davis was on her feet cheering throughout the game and some had asked her to stop blocking their view of the court. His attorney says Axelrod will sue the Davises for slander and seek $1 million.

With last season's brawl involving the Detroit Pistons, the Indiana Pacers, and many Pistons fans still echoing throughout the league, the NBA suspended Antonio Davis for five games—that'll cost him about $700,000 in salary—and said that five games was a light suspension, citing the mitigating circumstances, which Mr. Axlerod suggests are not so mitigating, at least as far as the misses are concerned.

In last year's melee, Ron Artest of Indiana was suspended for 73 games, teammate Steven Jackson for 30, and Jermaine O'Neal for 25, and they each also face criminal charges.

The most trenchant observation about this may have come from former NBA star, now TV analyst, Charles Barkley, who joined Dan Patrick and me on ESPN radio this afternoon. What the league should investigate, Barkley suggested, is why anybody was on their feet cheering wildly at a game between the 13-24 Knicks and the 16-22 Bulls.

We'll let the courts decide which of them deserves to be an Honorary Worst Person in the World.

Hotline to Heaven

The bronze goes to Kyle Cavanaugh, vice president of human resources at the University of Florida. The school's employees have a new health plan, under which they can enroll their wives, husbands, or domestic partners, provided they swear an affidavit that they are having sex with them. Mr. Cavanaugh says the school anticipates taking a long look at modifying the requirement.

Our runner-up: Frank Abramoff, the father of the pleaded-out lobbyist Jack Abramoff. He has responded to George Clooney's Golden Globes Award joke about the name "Jack Abramoff" in a letter to a Palm Springs newspaper. In the letter, he calls Clooney's joke "a lapse of lucidity" and an "obscene query." Q-U-E-R-Y. He also defends his son as a "fine man."

But the winner . . .

Reverend Prophet Ron Williams of the Miracle of Prayer Church in Grove Hill, Alabama.

His secretary was arrested and jailed last week. Williams went to the jail and demanded her release. Deputies say he caused a near riot, and, in the middle of it, he warned one of the deputies to leave him alone, pointed to his cell phone and said, "I got Johnny Cochran on the phone right now."

Johnny Cochran died last March.

Reverend Prophet Ron Williams, *today's* *Worst Person in the World!*

Jesus Wept

First there's Tyrone Burgo of Brockton, Massachusetts. Police say he posted an advertisement offering to sell cocaine. Online. And he listed a phone number.

The runner-up: The unnamed nurse at a hospital in Kyoto, Japan, sentenced to nearly four years in jail for trying to work off her stress by picking nails. Unfortunately those nails were the ones on the toes and fingers of six comatose and immobilized patients.

Thank goodness she wasn't biting her nails.

But the winner . . .

As equal-opportunity kvetches, we'll let you pick who you like least in this little soap opera:

Reverend Enrico Righi wrote in his church bulletin in the Italian town of Bagnoregio that Jesus Christ existed. A local atheist named Luigi Cascioli promptly filed a complaint with police, noting that saying Jesus existed, unless proven in court, violated two Italian national laws. So next week, Father Righi's lawyers have to go before a judge and prove Jesus Christ was a historical figure.

Your choice:

__Reverend Righi, Mr. Cascioli, the lawyers, the judge__, whichever nitwit is wasting Italian taxpayers' money on this hearing, today's Worst Person in the World!

The Other Big Giant Head

JANUARY 24, 2006

There's a sports theme to these.

The bronze: To referee John Hampton of college basketball's Conference USA. He'd just had it the other night with melodramatic coaches, when, after a foul call went against his team, University of Houston coach Tom Penders pretended to collapse in a heap on the sideline. Hampton called a technical foul on Penders and gave Alabama–Birmingham two free shots. The snag was, Coach Penders really had collapsed in a heap on the sideline. He has a heart condition and was wheeled off on a stretcher.

And the referees did not reverse their call!

Runner-up: John Kelly, a teacher at Beaver Area Senior High School in Beaver Falls, Pennsylvania. We think he's still a teacher.

It's Pittsburgh Steelers country there. Friday was a big day, what with the Steelers' playoff game against the Denver Broncos just 48 hours away. When student Joshua Vannoy showed up in class wearing a Broncos jersey, Mr. Kelly called Joshua a "stinking Denver fan," made Joshua sit on the floor, and encouraged other students to throw crumpled-up paper at him. "If he felt uncomfortable," said the teacher, "then that's a lesson; that's what the class is designed to do."

So if Mr. Kelly gets fired and banned from teaching for life, will that be his reaction?

But the winner . . .

Barry Bonds. When named last week to the USA team for the upcoming World Baseball Classic, Bonds was ecstatic about it. Then yesterday he suddenly pulled out of the tournament, saying, "I can't take any chances that might jeopardize my season."

Chances? Like what? Like the Olympic-style testing they're going to do, of all players, for . . . steroids?

Barry Bonds, *today's Worst Person in the World!*

"O'Reilly Has Really Gone Bonkers."

JANUARY 25, 2006

The bronze to Britain's Ministry of Defence. It made a big deal today about the fact that, with the younger of the British princes, Harry, joining the "Blues and Royals" Regiment, he could wind up being deployed to Iraq. They did not make such a big deal out of the other assignment possibility.

That Harry could be forced to guard Queen Elizabeth. His own grandma.

The runner-up: The fashion industry in Russia, the Czech Republic, and other Eastern European countries. The British Humane Society says its undercover investigation has produced videotape evidence that a lot of the fur of Eastern European origin in jacket collars and coats is from dogs and cats.

But the winners . . .

The folks at the special-interest group Accuracy in Media. Their latest harangue is about a news organization that isn't conservative enough for them. Directed at an outfit it claims gave Robert Kennedy Jr. a platform for an "environmental propaganda piece" about global warming. Against a network whose reporters let New Orleans "get to them." Against people "drifting to the left."

Fox News Channel.

No, seriously. To the left of whom? Vlad the Impaler?

One of AIM's e-mailers did, however, observe, "O'Reilly has really gone bonkers." So anyway, that's unanimous.

Accuracy in Media, *today's Worst Persons in the World!*

Bill and Payne

The bronze goes to Don Petrille, chairman of the Bucks County, Pennsylvania, Federation of Young Republicans. He's objecting to the sign in the front window of the county Democratic headquarters that reads "We Honor Our Fallen Heroes." Mr. Petrille is bothered by the fact that the Democrats use the sign to update the number of fatalities in Iraq. He says, "It ignores all the accomplishments we made in Iraq, such as eliminating the torture rooms, we overthrew Saddam Hussein . . ."

Next time you read that list, you might want to skip the "eliminating torture" part.

Our silver to an unnamed flight attendant from Northwest Airlines. She was arrested at Mitchell International Airport in Milwaukee after screeners discovered something in her carry-on bag. A hand grenade. It was real, although it was inactive. She explained she bought it at an army surplus store as a present for her son.

Well, as long as she had a good reason.

But the winner . . .

Mr. Bill. His latest triumph? A TV interview with Ms. Georgia Payne, identified as a "professional dominatrix." Their topic: the pressing, urgent problem of dominatrixes whose clients die on them. He explained that the risks of kinky sex made him worried for Ms. Payne, though, "If it were just you sitting with some guy discussing whatever you want to discuss, there's no problem."

Hmmm—this rings a distant bell—Bill O'Reilly, about women just talking dirty with some guy, it would be no prob—Ohhhhhh . . . yeaahhhhhhhhh . . .

Right, talking dirty. No problem at all. As long as you can pay that surcharge. Ten million dollars.

Bill O'Reilly, *today's Worst Person in the World!*

Ripped from Yesterday's Headlines

The bronze: The Ford Motor Company. As of next Wednesday, the only employees who will be able to park in the lot next to its truck plant in Dearborn, Michigan, are ones driving Fords. Can't imagine how that company got screwed up.

The silver for another "joke" from Ann Coulter. She told an audience at Philander Smith College in Arkansas last night that "we need somebody to put rat poisoning in Justice Stevens' creme brulee," then added, "That's just a joke, for you in the media." OK, here's another one.

I'm not sure Ann Coulter doesn't work for Osama Bin Laden. That's just a joke, for you in the media.

Speaking of jokes, the winner . . .

Him again. He has now ripped us here at MSNBC for not covering the case of Judge Edward Cashman of Vermont, who sentenced a serial child rapist to 60 days in jail.

Here's the thing, Bill. The Judge Cashman story from Vermont? We covered it here on *Countdown* on January 6 of this year. You didn't start until January 9.

He walked right into a propeller again.

Once again . . .

Bill O'Reilly, *today's Worst Person in the World!*

Not Anymore

The bronze to the German judge known only as Wolfgang W. He was about to sentence a robber to 22 months in prison when he met the defendant's girlfriend. They went out to dinner. And whatever her motives were, the next thing you knew, Judge Wolfgang was offering to send the guy up the river for much longer than 22 months—whatever the girlfriend wanted.

The runner-up: Luis Gabriel Cisneros. Police have broken an international counterfeiting ring because he gave four fake hundred-dollar bills to somebody who immediately knew they were fake. The Anaheim, California, stripper who'd just given him a three-hour lap dance.

But our winner . . .

The visitor to the Fitzwilliam Museum in Cambridge, England. The unnamed man tripped over his own shoelace and then came tumbling down a staircase into a display featuring three museum artifacts. To paraphrase one of the Inspector Clouseau movies:
"Those are priceless Ming Dynasty vases from China."
"Not anymooooore."

The lucky-they're-not-giving-out-his-name visitor to the museum in England, today's Worst Person in the World!

Deconstructing Bill

We have to go a little out of traditional sequence here because Bill O'Reilly is at it again.

For the second time in four shows, he whined about "cheap-shots" from MSNBC and NBC. This time he opened his program with it, ostensibly starting with a patronizing update on the health of ABC's Doug Vogt and Bob Woodruff, whom he identified as "Woodris."

There was a lot of guff about the "code among most in TV news of respect and professional courtesy," but most of what O'Reilly was saying was his typical obtuse shorthand of bullying—and another word starting with bull.

As a public service, I'm going to read portions of his remarks, and then translate them into what he's actually saying. The bottom line is, as the oldest cliche goes, he can dish it out, but he clearly cannot take it.

"Fox News has good relationships with ABC News, CBS News and generally CNN . . ."

That's probably why Fox bought those billboards across the street from CNN headquarters taunting them about ratings. Or issued the anonymous statement comparing CNN to the *Titanic*. Or the one about Ted Turner losing his mind.

"But Talking Points is troubled by the behavior of NBC, which cheap shots Fox News on a regular basis, and has been doing so for some time."

You know, I gotta confess, it never occurred to me before. But when we quote your own words back to you, about how the Catholic church was out to get Christmas or how we should let Al Qaeda attack San Francisco, they must seem like cheap shots.

"It is only a few people doing this, but NBC president Robert Wright allows it to happen. Wright knows exactly what's going on, because he's been made aware of it."

Maybe he hasn't, Bill. Mr. Wright is the chairman, not the president. So your postcard of complaint may have gone to the wrong office. And by the way, let us leave our bosses out of this, Bill, or I will have to call yours. And you know how much Satan hates to be disturbed while *American Idol* is on.

By the way, I ain't *callin'* Rupert Murdoch the devil.

"Now we understand that NBC has major problems. Its prime-time programming is dead last, its cable operations are ratings failures . . ."

In the cable ratings for the year 2005, USA Network, owned by NBC, finished three full places ahead of Fox News. And as to MSNBC, since February of 2005, our ratings tell an interesting story. In what was described today by NewsCorp as "the money demo," *Countdown*'s ratings are up 34 percent, but O'Reilly's have shriveled by 21 percent. Bill's obviously among our new viewers.

"But that is no excuse for unprofessional behavior."

Unless, that is, the unprofessional behavior is with one of your women producers, on the phone.

"There is no question the amazing success of Fox News has affected all TV news operations . . ."

Like bird flu.

" . . . but CNN, for example, usually competes with class, not bitterness."

Which is why we at Fox News compared CNN's Paula Zahn to an outhouse, and a dead muskrat.

"Likewise we respect ABC and CBS for their work ethic and competitive zeal."

Especially since David Letterman kicked the crap out of me on CBS earlier this month.

"But there's something very wrong at NBC. And if it continues, Talking Points will go into greater detail about the problems besetting that network."

Is this that "code among most in TV news of respect and professional courtesy" you mentioned, or do we get to that later?

"We hope Robert Wright will right the situation, and believe he has the power to do it. But perhaps we're wrong about Wright."

Bill made a funny. Heeeeee!

"Maybe he's out of the loop. Or maybe he just doesn't care. Well, he should care. We'll let you know what happens."
This is Ted Baxter, WJM. Good night . . . and good news!

Bill O'Reilly, *today's Worst Person in the World!*

Without personal
attacks, Bill, you'd
be a mime.

Masters Playing

The bronze: Judge Bruce Morgan from Telford, Shropshire, in England. He had accepted the explanation of a police constable, Mark Milton, that he was just "test driving" a new police car on the local M-54 motorway and needed to drive that fast to "familiarize himself" with what the car would do. Evidently it could do 159 miles an hour. Judge Morgan's ruling has been overruled, and Constable Milton will be tried after all.

The runner-up: Michael Caputo. Police in Indianapolis say he is the most wanted man in the city. The dreaded Manhole Cover Thief. They're charging him with stealing two, but they think he's stolen 51. Mr. Caputo is to be considered armed and heavily, well, armed. Big ripped arms from lifting manhole covers.

But the winner . . .

The gold goes to 32 percent of the male readers of *Golf Digest* and 31 percent of the female readers of *Golf For Women*. They responded "yes" to this survey question: If they let you play a round at Augusta National Golf Club, where they hold the Masters Tournament, would you be willing to, for that privilege, abstain from sex for a year?

That would obviously bring a whole new meaning to "Masters Playing."

Those readers of the two golf mags, *today's Worst Persons in the World!*

The First Rule of Forgery

FEBRUARY 2, 2006

Number three: It's Ted Baxter again. This time? Because CNN's Christiane Amanpour said, "Iraq has basically turned out to be a disaster." O'Reilly says of Ms. Amanpour, "You can draw by that that she has a rooting interest" in it being a disaster. Well, no, you can't, not if you use human logic. Besides which, he wouldn't really take a swipe at CNN after saying, "CNN, for example, usually competes with class, not bitterness."

The runner-up: Jerry McKay, who was arrested in Inverness, Florida, for speeding, going 71 in a 40-mile-an-hour zone. Police say that's when they found that, like many bad drivers, he wasn't concentrating on the speedometer. He was doing something else as he drove.

Cooking up some crystal meth.

But the winner . . .

Julie Kay Russo of Van Buren, Arkansas. She's been arrested for forgery. She's accused of trying to cash a fake payroll check at the S & S Super-Stop. Hard to believe you could be "Worst Person" for simply forging a check. Then again, you haven't heard yet what tipped the cashier off. The business name on the check included the word "Independent," which Ms. Russo had spelled I-n-d-*a*--p-e-n-d-e-n-t. Indahhhhh pendant.

Rule one of successful forgery: You cannot be a bad speller.

Julie Kay Russo, *today's Worst Person in the World!*

Know Your Customer

The bronze: To another unnamed seller taking advantage of the lack of supervision that defines eBay. Somebody was trying to sell the soul of the whale that died after mistakenly swimming up London's River Thames two weeks ago. "I was accompanying the poor whale in his last journey," the listing noted, "and he handed his soul to me." It might be believable, except the whale was a female.

Our runner-up: An unnamed pedestrian in Wittenberg, Wisconsin, arrested for twice *charging* moving cars. Getting down into a football stance, and then running right at them. Police had no trouble finding the guy. He was naked.

But the winner . . .

Another extry-special dumb criminal, Michael Garibay. He's under arrest in Orlando on charges of trying to sell cocaine. To a sheriff's deputy. Not an undercover sheriff's deputy. A guy in a uniform. And in his squad car!

Michael Garibay, *today's Worst Person in the World!*

Scenic Overlook

The bronze goes to Duncan Robinson of the Fitzwilliam Museum in Cambridge, England. You'll remember that's where three rare Chinese vases were destroyed, two weeks ago, when a patron of the arts fell down a staircase and crashed into them. Mr. Robinson has written to the vase-breaker, Nick Flynn, asking him not to visit the museum again in the future, even though, as Mr. Flynn points out, the vases were not tied down or protected in any way. "They were just left lying on the window sill."

The runner-up: Brooke Lord, spokeswoman for Melbourne Airport in Australia. She says the facility is still looking at legal action in the case of Stephen McKenzie-McHarg. He was fined $66 last summer for spending slightly more than 30 seconds in a pick-up lane, loading the six suitcases of his wife and daughter. Mr. McKenzie-McHarg has only one arm.

But the winners . . .

Big Outdoors and the Hustler Club. They've got a billboard in North Bergen, New Jersey, featuring a giant photo of a blond exotic dancer. It happens. It's America, 2006. But this billboard happens to overlook the playground at McKinley Elementary School.

Oops.

Big Outdoors and the Hustler Club*, today's Worst Persons in the World!*

Fill a Need

The bronze: Mike Holmgren, coach of the Seattle Seahawks. He told the 15,000 fans at the rally after Seattle lost the Super Bowl, "We knew it was going to be tough going up against the Pittsburgh Steelers. I didn't know we were going to have to play the guys in the striped shirts as well." It was a reference, of course, to the dubious refereeing. Fair enough, perhaps, except that Mr. Holmgren is also the team's vice president for football operations and a member of the NFL Competition Committee, which oversees rules and rules changes—and refereeing.

The silver: Deputy Jack Munsey of Martin County, Florida. Deputy Munsey is appealing his firing. The sheriff dismissed him after determining that Munsey spent some of his off hours at the beach, using his sheriff's vehicle dashboard-mounted camera to videotape women in bikinis, including one taking a shower.

But the winner . . .

Akmed Abu Dayya. He runs a store called The PLO Flag Shop, a souvenir stand of sorts in Gaza City.

Now many of us in the West may think that some of the Muslim reaction to those controversial Danish political cartoons has at last some justification. But, boy, it's hard to maintain that open-mindedness when you hear that after the rioting began, Mr. Abu Dayya contacted his wholesaler in Taiwan and ordered 100 Danish and Norwegian flags, which he sold to protestors so they could burn them.

Akmed Abu Dayya, *today's Worst Person in the World!*

Enemies List

FEBRUARY 7, 2006

Dozens of American journalists and politicians wound up in jail after the Adams administration passed the Alien and Sedition Acts in 1798, stifling political protest and creating the nation's first transgressors' list.

Nearly 2,000 who refused to name names before the House Un-American Activities Committee were rendered unemployable in Hollywood after the self-imposed blacklist of the 1950s.

And two decades after that, there was President Nixon's enemies list, posed with the goal of making difficult, by means of things like IRS audits, the lives of anyone thought to be against the Nixon White House.

So you haven't really made it into the Museum of Malignant American Political History until you've created your own list. Karl Rove may have just made it, as congressional sources told the conservative digest *Insight* that Mr. Rove has been twisting arms to ensure that the Senate Judiciary Committee's investigation of the domestic spy program does not bear any fruit, threatening any Republican member of the Senate who dares buck the administration's authorization of domestic wiretaps without warrants.

The iron fist inside the glove—that any straying lawmaker running for reelection in November could no longer count on any support from the White House. The assumption there being, of course, that come November, any Republican running for reelection will still want said president's help.

***Karl Rove**, today's Honorary Worst Person in the World!*

Who Was the Signatory?

The bronze: To the Bahamas Ministry of Tourism, which put a series of ads in the subways in New York encouraging riders to pretend they were on vacation by doing things like fishing on the tracks or stretching out over two or three seats. This, after a rider was discovered "stretched out" over two or three seats last month because he was dead. The ads have been removed.

Our runner-up: George C. Deutsch, one of the president's appointees at NASA, the one involved in trying to silence the scientists who tried to discuss global warming in public, or the Big Bang. He's resigned. Turned out he'd padded his resume, said he had a journalism degree from Texas A & M University. In fact he never graduated.

Wait a minute. You had to pretend to have a degree in journalism or communications?

But the winners . . .

Your federal government, and the Wachovia Bank in St. Leo, Florida. One of the checking accounts at the bank had a big problem. It tripped the kind of red flags that set terror watchdogs' hearts a-fluttering. The signatory to the account had no social security number or photo ID on file, so the bank froze the account and did not tell the account holders. Their checks started bouncing. They called the bank. And were told their assets had been frozen under provisions of the Patriot Act.

The account was in the name of the nuns at the Holy Name Monastery. The bank has apologized.

Denying money to possible terrorist Nuns . . .

Your federal government and the Wachovia Bank in St. Leo, Florida, today's *Worst Persons in the World!*

The Crowd Really Did Go Wild

Bronze: Fox News Channel. This morning, after the president's tale about breaking up a terror plot to destroy the Library Tower in Los Angeles, Fox illustrated its coverage by showing clips from the 1996 movie *Independence Day* that simulate the destruction of the Library Tower by intergalactic aliens.

Look, if you're going to whore out your channel to scare people on the president's behalf, at least save the *Independence Day* clips for when he claims he's only been eavesdropping on terrorist calls from Outer Space.

The runner-up: This yutz Glenn Beck again. After former president Carter's eulogy at the Coretta Scott King funeral, Beck announced on his radio show, "Is there a bigger waste of skin than Jimmy Carter?" Beck is the guy to whom CNN just gave a TV show, claiming he'll conduct a "conversation, not a confrontation."

Punt. Punt now.

But the winners . . .

Back to these guys. At Mrs. King's funeral, after Reverend Lowery made his remarks that "we know now there were no weapons of mass destruction" in Iraq, those in attendance gave him a 23-second standing ovation. When Fox News Channel ran the tape of Lowery's remark, it cut the applause to nine seconds.

And then Fox commentator Morton Kondracke came on and said: "The crowd did not go as wild as you—as it sounded as though it did at the time, and as various people have represented." He was surprised there wasn't more applause. After they *edited out* the applause!

Come on, it's journalism. Look it up in a dictionary.

Fox News Channel, *today's Worst Persons in the World!*

If Only a Pigeon Were Driving the Bus

FEBRUARY 10, 2006

The bronze: Kimberly Lynn DaSilva of Boston. The FBI says the former strip-club waitress believed herself mistreated by men. So she took some condoms and made them into potential mini-bombs by filling them with drain cleaner and gasoline. She then mailed them to strip clubs and a Boston TV station.

Hey, I used to work for a Boston TV station, so although I would never condone exploding-condom mailing, I believe I understand it.

Our runner-up: Renee Cipriano. Six months ago, she was the director of the Illinois Environmental Protection Agency, fighting to tighten mercury pollution regulations for the state's utilities. Today, she is a lobbyist for Ameren, owners of a bunch of Illinois power companies, fighting to loosen mercury pollution regulations for the state's utilities. Good to be flexible.

But the winner . . .

Mario Edney, municipal bus driver in the city of Philadelphia. Ralph Kramden he is not. Authorities say when a passenger complained Edney had bypassed her stop, he grabbed her, knocked her head into that pole next to his seat, opened his front door, and threw her out onto the pavement.

Well, it does say you're not supposed to talk to the driver.

Courteous, professional, willing to throw you under his own bus . . .

Mario Edney, *today's Worst Person in the World!*

Dear Editor

The bronze to Ann Coulter. Calling Muslims "ragheads" in a speech to the Conservative Political Action Conference in Washington would ordinarily be very offensive, except the degree of difficulty for Ann has dropped over the years. Now when she says something offensive and clever, she'll score higher.

Our runner-up: William Donohue, the president of the Catholic League for Religious and Civil Rights, or, as he likes to call it, simply "the Catholic League." Complaining again that Hollywood producers and performers are destroying America, he said that some of them "will do anything for the buck. They wouldn't care. If you asked them to sodomize their own mother in a movie, they would do so, and they would do it with a smile on their face."
I wanna know which films this guy's been watching . . .

But the winner . . .

Mel Hooker, human resources chief of the Veterans Affairs agency. A woman in New Mexico wrote a letter to the editor, as a private citizen, evidently on her own time, away from work. It was published in a weekly newspaper in Albuquerque. Laura Berg strongly criticized President Bush and his administration for its handling of Iraq and Katrina, and suggested that the country "act forcefully" to impeach and/or prosecute.
Mr. Hooker, the V.A. HR chief, discovered that Ms. Berg was a nurse in a V.A. hospital, so he ordered his agency to seize her office computer and investigate her. Says he has to investigate "any act which potentially represents sedition."
Sedition? Who do you think you are, pal? President John Adams? Trotsky? Sedition! For writing a letter to the editor!

***Mel Hooker**, today's Worst Person in the World!*

She Said She Was the Original Blonde

FEBRUARY 15, 2006

The bronze to whoever stole a business ad sign from a company in Crystal River, Florida. It was outside the Advanced Family Hearing Center. A four-foot-tall fiberglass ear. There were two of them, but now, says manager Amy Wylde, "one of them's gone."

Maybe it wasn't stolen. Maybe it's just been borrowed. You know, "lend me your ear."

Our runner-up: Olympic management at the Adidas sporting goods company. It made a deal to outfit the German Olympic ski team and proceeded to deliver to them, in Turin, 30 caps bearing the colors of Belgium. Not Germany, Belgium. The country Germany rolled through at the start of both world wars. A lot of Belgian ghosts laughing it up big-time.

But our winner . . .

Ann Coulter! When she took the bronze earlier this week, we suggested she needed to be creative to do better. She's been creative. The *Palm Beach Post*, quoting voting records from Palm Beach County, Florida, indicated that in last week's county council election she voted in Precinct 1196, about four miles north of her home. Applause that she voted in a local election. Except she was supposed to vote in Precinct 1198, the precinct in which her home stands.

Florida law makes it a third-degree felony to knowingly vote in the wrong precinct. Violators can be fined up to five grand and go to jail for five years. So stay tuned for Ann's unexpectedly passionate plea for prison reform.

Ann Coulter, *today's Worst Person in the World!*

Irony Is Reborn

FEBRUARY 16, 2006

The bronze: to Detective Inspector Stephen Clay of Scunthorpe in England. He pulled up to a traffic light, alongside motorist Valerie Smith. She could see he had something in his hand. Detective Inspector Clay says it was his mobile phone. Mrs. Smith says it was part of his anatomy. Clay claims he was just "scrolling through the calendar."

Well, I've heard a lot of euphemisms for it, but that's a new one.

Our runner-up, part of a Dick Cheney Fall-Out mini-theme: Deer hunters in Germantown, Maryland, who were called in to "cull the herd" in a 206-acre piece of property. A hunting club? No, no, the grounds of the local, nondenominational Christian Church of the Savior, whose members are committed to the environment.

But our winner . . .

Josh Kayser of Lafayette, Colorado. He was reflecting on the Cheney shooting incident, he confesses. "I said to myself, 'How can you shoot your friend with your gun?'" It was at that point, as they hunted raccoons on his family's property, that his 17-year-old girlfriend accidentally shot him in the head. Superficial injuries.

Fortunately, from her ranch in South Texas, Mrs. Katharine Armstrong saw the whole thing, so there will be no charges.

***Josh Kayser**, today's Worst Person in the World!*

I Hear They Are Calling

FEBRUARY 17, 2006

The bronze: Jennifer Silva, a teacher in Katy, Texas. She told her class that if they didn't settle down, she'd tape their mouths shut with Scotch tape. They didn't. She did. She's been suspended.

Our runner-up tonight: Environmental protestors in Turin, Italy. To try to combat global warming, they want less fuel used on the Olympic torch.

We know you're right. Just give it a rest till next week, huh?

But the winner . . .

Former baseball star Albert Belle. The global positioning satellite device on the car of his ex-girlfriend fell off late last month. This was a double shock to her, insofar as she'd never put a GPS device on her car. It did explain why the former slugger kept showing up at the store she was shopping at, or the gym, or on her dates with other guys. Belle is charged with stalking, out on bail of $108,000.

He also gets bonus points for telling an Associated Press writer, "You didn't write a story about my Hall of Fame induction. You guys never report the good stuff that I do."

Albert, hate to break it to you, but you didn't get inducted into the Hall of Fame this year.

Albert Belle, *today's Worst Person in the World!*

Hero Librarian

FEBRUARY 20, 2006

The bronze, the only civilian of the three: An 18-year-old senior in the theater group of the L. D. Bell High School in Hurst, Texas. She was understudying a sophomore in the school play. She really wanted the part. She bought the girl a Mountain Dew. The girl smelled something funny and got a teacher. The understudy had spiked the soda with bleach. We'll call the senior . . . Eve Harrington.

The runner-up: Harold Hurtt, the police chief of Houston. He says the city should be blanketed with surveillance cameras, including in apartment complexes and private homes. You can make the argument, but not by saying what he said: "I know a lot of people are concerned about Big Brother, but my response to that is if you are not doing anything wrong, why should you worry about it?"

Because, Big Brother Hurtt, I'd like to remind you that the definition of "doing anything wrong" can change from time to time.

As an example, the winners . . .

Two members of the Homeland Security Department of Montgomery County, Maryland. They actually walked in to a public library there in Bethesda last Friday and announced to the patrons that the viewing of internet pornography was forbidden. One of them actually went up to a guy at a computer and challenged the Web site he was at, and asked the man to step outside.

A librarian intervened. One who had actually read the constitution, evidently. The police were called. The two Homeland Security zealots were escorted from the library.

The Homeland Security zealots of Montgomery County, *today's Worst Persons in the World!*

Nobody with Brains

The bronze: An unnamed mother in League City, Texas. She dropped her 6-year-old daughter off at elementary school. The girl was improperly dressed, considering it was chilly and drizzling. And it was Saturday. And Mom didn't notice that there was no school. Even though there were no cars in the parking lot, or kids in the area. She's been arrested.

The runner-up: Lecturers Edwina Luck and Dr. Yunus Ali of the Queensland University of Technology business school. Student Rohan Duggan submitted a paper in Ms. Luck's class. She didn't like his grammar. Marked up the paper with a note suggesting Duggan needed to do "more smarter writing." After that, he asked to have another teacher look at the paper. That was when Dr. Ali saw it and gave him a *lower* grade, complaining that he referred to two guys whom he didn't mention as references in the bibliography, "Yin" and "Yang."

But the winner . . .

Senator Orrin Hatch of Utah. In a speech defending warrant-free domestic spying, he pointed out that things were going well in Iraq because "we've stopped a mass murderer in Saddam Hussein. Nobody denies that he was supporting Al Qaeda. Well, I shouldn't say nobody. Nobody with brains." Gee, who were those guys who denied it? Some kind of 9/11 Commission?

Always important to remember, senator, that just because somebody like you might have brains, that doesn't mean they aren't in your backside.

Senator Orrin Hatch, *today's Worst Person in the World!*

When Bills Attack

The bronze: To the operators of a fertilizer plant in the Bavarian village of Elsa, Germany. The main tank burst. The picturesque village was soon 20 inches deep in pig manure.

Speaking of which, the runner-up: Last night's winner, Senator Orrin Hatch of Utah, who had said of Saddam Hussein, "Nobody denies that he was supporting Al Qaeda. Well, I shouldn't say nobody. Nobody with brains." He's now trying to spin out of that. He says he may have misspoken, saying he meant not that Saddam Hussein supported Al Qaeda, but that the post-Saddam insurgency was being supported by Al Qaeda and Abu Musab Al-Zarqawi.

"Misspeaking" is calling the Library Tower the Liberty Tower. You might as well now claim you were actually giving the Olympic hockey scores in code.

But the winner . . .

Oh! He's baaaack. Ted Baxter has called for the firing of one of his own network's commentators. The eminent author and journalist Neal Gabler appears on *Fox News Watch*, the only show on that network that actually tries to live up to the catchphrase "fair and balanced." But O'Reilly, on the same network, called Gabler a "rabid dog" who "traffics in personal attacks."

Can we just drop this whining about "personal attacks," Billy? Without personal attacks, you'd be a mime.

Bill O'Reilly . . . *you know the rest.*

Pinhead

FEBRUARY 23, 2006

The bronze goes to H. Lee Scott Jr. He's the chief executive of the ever-popular Wal-Mart company. In what he thought was a secure online chat with company managers, one of them asked why "the largest company on the planet cannot offer some type of medical retirement benefits." Mr. Scott explained how costly that would be and then suggested that the manager was disloyal and might want to look for a new job.

The runner-up: Rush Limbaugh. Complaining about a story that noted Ruth Bader Ginsburg is the only woman on the Supreme Court, he said if she didn't like it, she should resign, and then he added, "Besides, David Souter's a girl. Everybody knows that. What's the big deal? I'm talking about attitudinally, here, folks."

But the winner . . .

Ohhhh, it's two in a row for Ted Baxter! You may recall that last November, on the *Today Show*, for God's sake, he said that people who favored a quick or immediate withdrawal from Iraq were "pinheads" and compared them to those who had wanted to appease Adolf Hitler.

Now he says of our role in Iraq: "The only solution to this is to hand over everything to the Iraqis as fast as humanly possible. Because we can't control these crazy people."

Bill, now you know how your employers feel.

Bill O'Reilly, *today's Worst Person in the World!*

Graphic Idiocy

The bronze: To a judge in the nation of Colombia. He found a bicycle courier guilty of groping a woman's backside. Fair enough. We're not defending groping backsides of any gender or religious conviction. But the guy gave the groper four years in jail.

The silver: Kevin Murphy, deputy commissioner of the Minnesota Department of Commerce. He has levied a fine of $140,000 against a gas station chain, Midwest Oil, because of the price it charged customers for a gallon of gas on 293 different days last year.
    The fine is for selling the gas too cheaply.

But the winner . . .

The staff of *Your World with Neil Cavuto* on Fox News. Yesterday they analyzed the destruction of the Golden Mosque and the resultant murders of dozens of Iraqi civilians, describing all of it with this on-screen graphic: "All-out Civil War in Iraq: Could It Be A Good Thing?"

The staff of Your World with Neil Cavuto,
today's Worst Persons in the World!

Incredibility

The bronze goes to Mark Reynier, chairman of the Bruichladdich Distillery in Scotland. Today, it turned out twelve barrels of whiskey, according to a recipe unused since the seventeenth century. The stuff is 92 percent alcohol. Three years ago, our Secret Service admitted that it had been monitoring the distillery, because the difference between distilling high-alcohol whiskey and making chemical weapons was "just a small tweak."

The silver to the international soccer star David Beckham. He says he's struggling to help his son with his math homework. His son is 6 years old. Says Mr. Posh Spice: "It's done totally differently to what I was teached when I was at school."

So that remark also takes care of any grammar homework Beckham Junior may get.

But the winner . . .

Yeah, him again. On the air, he actually reproached his guest Mike Farrell: "You lose credibility when you use personal attacks." Mr. Farrell pointed out that Billy might have discovered that some gain credibility using them. To which O'Reilly replied, "I don't do personal attacks here, mister. We don't do personal attacks."

Other than calling Neal Gabler a "rabid dog" and Ralph Nader a "loon" and Bill Moyers a "fanatic" and Barbara Boxer a "nut" and Jimmy Carter a "fool" and John Kerry a "sissy." Got a suggestion, Bill. Start another petition. Demand that somebody give you back your credibility.

Bill O'Reilly, *today's Worst Person in the World!*

Stunned

FEBRUARY 27, 2006

He was an overnight celebrity at the age of 83, turned into one of the faces of baseball by the Ken Burns documentary. Buck O'Neil, a living link to the great stars who had been prevented from reaching the major leagues because of the color barrier that would not fall until 1947. Himself, Jackie Robinson's teammate with the legendary Kansas City Monarchs, later their manager.

Even at the age of 94, Buck O'Neil remains one of the great ambassadors in any sport, but now baseball might as well have told him to get lost. This was the day the game elected to its Hall of Fame 17 heroes from the era of the Negro leagues, the last such election scheduled, ever, and Buck O'Neil was not elected.

A special committee first selected 94 candidates, then pared them down to 39 finalists, and today announced the 17 inductees. O'Neil did not make the cut, nor did Minnie Minoso, himself prevented from playing in the majors until he was 27 years old because of the color of his skin. Minoso, playing mostly with the Chicago White Sox, went on to record the sixth highest batting average in all of baseball during the prime of his career, 1951 through 1963.

Snubbing Minoso and O'Neil apparently for all time is extraordinary enough, but only baseball could make it worse. In honoring the Negro leagues, it managed to exclude O'Neil and Minoso, but it did elect two white people. James Leslie Wilkinson was the founder of those Kansas City Monarchs, Jackie Robinson's team before he broke the color barrier with the Brooklyn Dodgers. Wilkinson was a white businessman.

And today's election also made a Hall of Famer out of Effa Manley. She was the owner of the Newark Eagles of the Negro-American League. It sounds almost impossible to believe, but she too was white. She was married to a black man, the team's co-owner, and she pretended to, the term was then, pass as a light-skinned black woman. In addition, her husband reportedly traded away at least one of the team's players because she was having an affair with that player.

Most of the 17 electees today were entirely deserving. Such legendary figures as Sol White and Bizz Mackey and Jose Mendez will achieve in death and in the Hall something they were denied in life.

But just to twist the knife a little further into Buck O'Neil, the special committee elected Alex Pompez, owner of the New York Cubans team in the 1930s and 1940s, also an organized crime figure—part of the mob of the infamous 1930s gangster Dutch Schultz—indicted in this country and in Mexico for racketeering. He's in the Hall of Fame for all time. Buck O'Neil is not.

Explanations from that committee, though, have been few and cowardly. One who did speak up who apparently had voted for Buck O'Neil was Ray Doswell, curator of the Negro League's museum.

"Honestly," he says, "Buck has a lot of fans on this committee, and I think even the people who didn't vote for him are his fans, but they decided to vote with their conscience and the high standards of the Hall of Fame."

Those high standards, by the way, permitted them to elect Pompez the gangster and Manley the adulteress who pretended to be black.

These were not the regular Hall of Fame voters but twelve so-called experts, at least eight of whom are, like me, members of the Society for American Baseball Research. Nine votes from them were required for election.

The voters were Todd Bolton; Greg Bond, who's associated with the University of Wisconsin; Adrian Burgos Jr., an assistant professor at the University of Illinois at Urbana-Champaign; Dick Clark; Ray Doswell, mentioned earlier; Leslie Heaphy, associated with Kent State; Dr. Larry Hogan from Union County College of New Jersey; Larry Lester; Sammy Miller; Jim Overmyer; the late Robert Peterson, who passed away just two weeks ago; and Rob Ruck.

I contacted seven of them by e-mail and got four replies today. Each refused a request to say even how they voted on Minoso or O'Neil. Mr. Overmyer wrote, "The members of this committee were specifically asked by the Hall not to talk about their choices, and I have to respect the implicit promise I made to the Hall when I took this assignment."

However, baseball's Hall of Fame tells us it only asked the voters not to talk about their choices yesterday, as those choices were first being revealed to the public. There is nothing restricting the voters from speaking publicly now; they just won't.

It's not merely indefensible. For all the many stupid things the baseball Hall of Fame has ever done, this is the worst.

Many of us erupted in anger. Jason Whitlock wrote in the *Kansas City Star*: "The Baseball Hall of Fame needed Buck O'Neil far more than Buck O'Neil needed the Baseball Hall of Fame." Cleveland Indians legend Bob Feller, who pitched against O'Neil 60 years ago, told the *Star*, "If I were him, I would be mad as hell. I'm going to have some words."

A Missouri congressman said on the floor of the House that the committee vote had "left a community in tears." The governor of Kansas brought up the subject to reporters without being asked. "I'm just sort of stunned," she said. And from inside the world of baseball historians, there are increasing indications that Buck O'Neil may have been the victim as much of politics as of voters who doubted his credentials. That powers at the National Baseball Hall of Fame may have resented his being involved in the Negro Leagues Museum.

But Buck himself did not erupt. He said the committee did its best, he was happy that so many of his peers and predecessors were finally given their due, and since all of them had already passed away, he volunteered to speak on their behalf at the induction ceremonies in Cooperstown, New York, this summer.

His is the standard to which the Hall should aspire.

***The twelve members of the Hall of Fame's special committee**, today's Honorary Worst Persons in the World!*

Factually Challenged

The bronze to Principal Mike Neece at Ramona High School in Riverside, California. Two seniors decided that what the school needed was a snowball fight. They drove to the San Bernardino Mountains to load up their pickups, drove the snow to the school, and were promptly suspended, because snowballs are considered dangerous.

Mr. Neece, you need a week in upstate New York.

The runners-up: Randy Beaty, Carlos Torres-Ramos, and Humberto Ponce, drivers on Highway 26 in Rock County, Wisconsin. You've probably thought, "Too bad drunk drivers don't crash into each other." Each was arrested after a four-car accident. Each charged with drunk driving.

But the winner . . .

Brit Hume from Fox News. At it again. Monday, he described Senate Democratic leader Harry Reid as "factually challenged" after Reid said Dubai Ports World was "taking control of our ports." Hume said they were not "getting control" of the ports. But as recently as last Wednesday, the situation was described thusly on Fox News: "The Bush administration was trying today to dig itself out of a political hole on the question of who should control some of the nation's ports."

Who used that word "control" and then criticized a Democrat for using the same word?

Brit Hume, *today's Worst Person in the World!*

Sane. That's one fella
Mr. O'Reilly has
apparently never met.

Grace under Fire

The bronze: Ferenc Orsos of Woonsocket, Rhode Island. His apartment caught fire, and when the firefighters showed up he attacked them. With a sword. Fortunately, the police showed up. With a stun gun. He's under arrest.

The runner-up: Fox News again. I mean, I'll say it again, I should send them a check every week for all the material they just hand us. An on-screen graphic today, during Neil Cavuto's show: "'Civil War' in Iraq: Made Up By The Media?"
Right. We made up all those dead Iraqis. And the blown-up mosque. Photoshopped.

But the winner . . .

Speaking of Photoshopped, Nancy Grace, of *CNN Headline News*. For years she has openly spoken of the murder of her fiancé when she was 19 years old, and how it set her off on her career path—whatever her career really is. She's always said the man was shot five times by a stranger with a long rap sheet, for the 35 bucks in his wallet, and that the murderer denied any involvement, and that she had to live through a series of painful appeals, and thus defense lawyers are devils.
The *New York Observer* reports today that the records show that Grace's fiancé was in fact shot by a former coworker with no prior convictions, who confessed the night he was arrested and didn't get the death penalty because he was mildly retarded, and oh, by the way, he never appealed his conviction.
Padding the story of the murder of your fiancé? Euuuuuuu . . .

Nancy Grace, *today's Worst Person in the World!*

One Crazy Mother

MARCH 2, 2006

There's Jacqueline Forbes of Brisbane, Australia. She's under arrest for leaving something at the salad bar at two of the Sizzler restaurants in that city: poison in the pasta sauce. Four diners got sick, but Sizzler still waited five weeks to report it to the police. Its restaurants in Brisbane have been virtually empty since Monday. Ownership closed all of them, yesterday.

The silver: To the Rug Doctor company of Windber, Pennsylvania. Last month, salesman Bernard Chippie called in from his route to say he would have to go home. Doctors had told his terminally ill wife that she was down to between two days and a week to live. So Rug Doctor fired him. They said he'd used up all his sick days and unpaid leave.

When the story got out, the company offered him his job back. Surprisingly enough, he's skeptical.

But the winner . . .

Melissa Cheeney of Pioche, Nevada. Police say she didn't like the refereeing in the basketball game for fifth and sixth graders in which her son was playing, so afterwards, she waited for the ref and promptly grabbed the official by the hair, knocked the ref to the ground, and started kicking the ref. The ref in this case was not only a woman, she was a woman who is five months pregnant.

She's okay. The crazy mother is under arrest.

And she's . . .

Melissa Cheeney, *today's Worst Person in the World!*

Party On, Wayne

MARCH 3, 2006

A theme of your tax-dollars in action.

The bronze: Mayor Ben Cooper of Wise, Virginia. He's also police supervisor and town manager, and one of 14 people charged with scheming to take over the town council through election fraud. Mayor Cooper's in the most trouble. The counts against him total 240.

Our silver: Mayor Bert Reeves of Cottageville, South Carolina, once a notorious speed trap. The mayor worked diligently to change the town's reputation. Wednesday he was pulled over for speeding: 103, in a 55-mile-an-hour zone.

But the winners:

The town aldermen of Aurora, Illinois. Still got your Christmas lights up? Your Halloween decorations? You can be fined. Fifty bucks. New law passed: decorations can go up 60 days before a holiday, must come down 60 days after it.

And what if I want to listen to Dickens and keep Christmas every day of the year? Huh? Huh? Didn't think of that, did ya, ya bastards!

The aldermen of Aurora, Illinois—*party on, Wayne— you're today's Worst Persons in the World!*

Window Dressing

The bronze: The wrecking crew in New York City that started demolishing a building in Queens. Residents woke up around 8 A.M. to a wrecking ball coming through the wall. The workers were destroying the wrong building.

The runner-up: Rush Limbaugh, on his radio show discussing the "Hillary Fear" that America should have of a Clinton run in '08. He said: "When she's genuine, she sounds like a screeching ex-wife. And—and—and I don't say that—there's nothing against ex-wives or women. I'm just trying to be descriptive here for you. Men will know what I mean by this."

Well, men like Rush who have ex-wives. Rush has three of them.

But the winner . . .

Officials at our Department of Homeland Security. Those at the actual building in Washington, to be exact.

Do you ever get the feeling that there's no real threat to homeland security, and that these guys know it, and that they just sit around all day dreaming up stuff to scare us with? Guards there report that last fall, an envelope with a suspicious white powder was opened at the headquarters, and rather than evacuate the building, an official carried the envelope to the office next door to Secretary Chertoff and shook the contents out the window.

Biological weapon? Hell's bells, it doesn't even slow the pedestrians down!

The Department of Homeland Security, *today's*
Worst Persons in the World!

Calling Plan

MARCH 8, 2006

At the bronze level: City officials of Cape Coral, Florida, who apparently did nothing to answer the repeated complaints of resident Robert Payne about the "public copulation" in the parking lot next to his house. Payne was so disgusted by the activity and the used contraceptives left behind that he picked them all up and planted a "condom garden" on the main street. He's got their attention now.

The runner-up: Deloris Smith, a hotel maid in Charleston, South Carolina. She's been arrested after a fight with another maid that started in the laundry room, reportedly over the last roll of toilet paper, and spilled out into the parking lot. Smith was armed with a mop, the other maid only had a plunger.

But the winner . . .

James R. Hood of Granville, Ohio. He's been arrested for making obscene phone calls in the middle of the night—2,623 of them in 20 days to random people in more than eight countries.

This sounds like a job for Fox Security!

James R. Hood, *today's Worst Person in the World!*

In a Sane World

MARCH 10, 2006

The bronze: Brandon Wilcox, a 25-year-old Arizona man arrested this week for DWI after he crashed his car into two curbs, abandoned it on the side of the road, and walked home, where police found him passed out with a blood alcohol level twice the legal limit. Nothing too unusual about that except that Wilcox is himself an Albuquerque police officer, and the car he crashed was his police cruiser.

The runner-up: Another peace officer, Deputy James Pruitt of Galveston, Texas. He was giving his 13-year-old nephew an unauthorized tour of the county jail and decided he'd teach the kid a lesson about his behavior. So he locked the kid in a jail cell with an accused murderer.

The lesson? Uncle Jim is an idiot.

But the winner:

Ted Baxter again, taking a break from threatening radio callers about me to instead threaten Iran. "You know," he said, "In a sane world, every country would unite against Iran and blow it off the face of the earth. That would be the sane thing to do." Which of course is how the Iranians feel about us, and we think they're nuts.

Sane. That's one fella Mr. O'Reilly has apparently never met. Now and forever . . .

Bill O'Reilly, *today's Worst Person in the World!*

Stuck in the Middle with You

MARCH 14, 2006

The bronze: Bill Schalow, county coordinator of Douglas County, Minnesota. He's apologized for this, for telling the local newspaper, the *Springfield Echo Press*, that henceforth all its stories about the county had to be submitted to him for fact-checking and approval, or no county official would ever speak to the paper again.

Somewhere, some exec at Fox News is snapping his fingers and saying, "Shucks!"

The runner-up: Televangelist Pat Robertson. Telling his by now benumbed TV audience that "the goal of Islam, ladies and gentlemen, whether you like it or not, is world domination." He later clarified this by saying he only meant radical Islamist extremists.

Details, shmetails, right?

But the winner . . .

Northwest Airlines. This was inevitable. The airline is now saying that on many of its flights, if you don't want to get stuck in that middle seat, that seven-inch-wide thing designed for really small third graders, it'll cost you an extra fifteen bucks. That's right: you want an aisle seat, you pay the blackmail. Fifteen dollars.

Coming soon: it'll cost you an extra three bucks per flight if you want to sit down!

Northwest Airlines, *today's Worst Persons in the World!*

Rush's Masterpiece

MARCH 15, 2006

The bronze goes to two guards from the Securicor Company. Their van, parked outside a bank in a town in Lampeter, Wales, began to shriek with sirens and prerecorded calls to get the police. The van was "under threat." The threat? The two Securicor guards had locked themselves inside the van. Took an hour to get them out.

Our runners-up: The doubters about global warming. Residents of the western part of South Korea were told to stay indoors or wear masks outside because that wasn't just snow falling from the sky. It was a mix of snow and yellow sand.

Kids, come in, it's sanding outside!

But the winner . . .

Comedian Rush Limbaugh. Another friendly word from the master of courteous political debate. Referring to our former colleague Claire Shipman, now an ABC News correspondent, and her husband Jay Carney, deputy Washington bureau chief of *Time* magazine, he said:

"Claire Shipman and Jay Carney are uh, slave owner and husband. Well, husband and wife, if you prefer that, and, and slave master. I take it back, slave master, not slave owner. Slave master and wife . . ."

Yes? Pharmacy? I'd like to order some refills for Mr. Limbaugh?

Rush Limbaugh, *today's Worst Person in the World!*

The Tighter They Squeeze

MARCH 15, 2006

An item you can put under that heading of post-9/11 thinking: Why let the terrorists destroy our freedoms when we can do it perfectly well ourselves?

It's the Pittsburgh perfect picture pickle. In 2002, the FBI monitored members of an anti-war group, the Thomas Merton Center in Pittsburgh, this according to documents released by the FBI under a Freedom of Information Act request made by the American Civil Liberties Union. The surveillance included photographs of an anti-war event on November 29, 2002. Do the math with me. That's four months before the war had even begun.

The once-secret FBI report from that date describes the Merton Center as a "left-wing organization advocating, among many political causes, pacifism," and that it "holds daily leaflet distribution activities and is currently focused on opposition to the potential war with Iraq."

Further, "There are more than a few Muslims and people of Middle Eastern descent among the regulars."

The FBI, through a statement, essentially says it was looking for one person only, and when the photos did not reveal that person, the photos were destroyed. But a draft letter by the FBI dated February 26, 2003, describes the Thomas Merton Center as an anti-war group under the title "International Terrorism Matters."

For fighting a war against those who don't want to fight a war . . .

The FBI, *today's Honorary Worst Persons in the World!*

Nosing Around

This time, actually, it's the worst animals in the world.

The bronze goes to the squirrels of LaCrosse, Wisconsin. Their presence at a celebration of the anniversary of the city's founding led to the prospect of the members of the Wisconsin Infantrymen, firing off the 21-gun salute, being fined for violating city ordinance number 381, "for the protection of squirrels within the city limits." The Mayor says if any tickets are issued, he'll pay them.

The runner-up: Another squirrel, this one in Mount Pleasant Township, Pennsylvania. It decided to cross the road—Route 116—and a motorist decided to stop, to avoid hitting it. He was promptly rear-ended by the motorist behind him. They were hit by a third car. All three were hit by a fourth. Nobody injured. The squirrel is laughing his acorns off.

But the winner . . .

An unnamed bomb-sniffing dog. Brought in to check out the Cox Arena at San Diego State University this morning before the NCAA Basketball Tournament games there. He smelled something. They wound up evacuating the place and delaying the first game by two hours. There was no bomb, no threat. The theory is, he smelled nitrates in one particular place.

To quote university spokesman Jack Beresford, "a bomb-sniffing dog noticed something in a hot dog cart."

Yeah, Snausages!

The hungry hungry bomb-sniffing pooch, *today's Worst Creature in the World!*

Tip of the Iceberg

MARCH 16, 2006

Sometimes criminals are so dumb they go from merely bad to worse.

An honorary bronze: Curtis Gokey of Lodi, California. A city dump truck backed into his car, causing about $3,600 in damages, so he sued, even though Mr. Gokey was the city employee driving the dump truck. He crashed into his own car. The suit was thrown out. So now instead, his wife has sued the city on his behalf.

An honorary silver: Gary Brunner of Carmel, New York, popped into the Putnam County sheriff's office and asked if there were any warrants outstanding for his own arrest. Amazed officers discovered there were, for drug trafficking. He was arrested. Apparently the first self-serve customer they've ever had there.

And the honorary winner?

Two thieves in Prince George, Canada, caught on surveillance tape robbing a local museum. They stole the museum's surveillance cameras. But they forgot to steal the tapes made by the surveillance cameras showing them stealing the surveillance cameras.

The museum thieves in Prince George:
Honorary Worst Persons in the World!

Whack Job

The bronze: John Dunleavy, chairman of today's New York St. Patrick's Day Parade. Oh heeere we go. This year's rationale for barring the Irish Lesbian and Gay Association from the Parade: "If an Israeli group wants to march in New York," he says, "do you allow neo-Nazis into their parade?" Boy, that's a good analogy.

The runner-up: Ted Baxter again, ripping his own Fox News colleague Neal Gabler again. Calling him a "bomb-thrower" and a "Kool-Aid drinker" because on the Fox media show, Gabler complained that a Colorado family had gone to the conservative media to complain about a high school teacher, rather than to the school. On the same show on which Gabler said that, his colleague Cal Thomas agreed with Gabler, but O'Reilly didn't call him a "Kool-Aid drinker."

But the winner . . .

We're celebrating the day with a double dose of Bill. Explaining to a caller, one of the ones who didn't get arrested, that he wouldn't denigrate a guest because that's why he has his co-host, Lis Wiehl. "Every time I want to do that," he said, "I just go over to her and whack her around. Figuratively speaking of course."

Yeah, figuratively speaking. Just hit her with a loofah, Billy.

Bill O'Reilly, *today's Worst Person in the World!*

Scouting Mission

The bronze: Diane Marcotte of Island Lake, Illinois. She was pulled over for drunk driving with her 3-year-old boy in the car. Bad, but fairly ordinary. Until the police added that also drunk in the car was Ms. Marcotte's 4-month-old Chihuahua.

Our runner-up: Edward Cuebas of Savannah. He celebrated St. Patrick's Day by urinating into the gas tank of a car. Again, bad, but fairly ordinary. Until the police added that the car he urinated into was a Savannah police car. A marked car. A black and white.

But the winners:

The two men who, before the president's trip to the Mississippi Coast the week before last, stopped by the home of Jerry Akins in the beachfront town of Gautier. They took pictures and asked questions and explained they were from Fox News. Doing a "scouting mission" for a story on reconstruction.

After the president stopped by Mr. Akins's home, the two men, says Akins, came back in to say, sorry, they weren't with Fox News, they were actually part of the governmental entourage.

Fox News reporters. Who are actually federal agents. You know, you're just making this too easy for me. Anyway, if you're worried about the journalistic ethics involved here, don't. The people at Fox News pretend to be journalists every day.

***Two unidentified federal agents**, today's*
Worst Persons in the World!

Off-line

MARCH 21, 2006

The bronze: Annie's back. She has titled her column criticizing all the attention paid to the arrest of former Domestic Policy Advisor Claude Allen, "Revenge of the Queers."

How'd you like to try to be her lawyer at a sanity hearing?

The runner-up: Albert Coleman Jr. The 61-year-old substitute teacher will spend a year on probation after reprimanding an 8-year-old by making him stand on a chair, looping around his neck a piece of decorative string that was loosely attached to a light fixture, and then kicking the chair. Mr. Coleman said, well, the string was never around the boy's neck. The state said, well, great, you can't be a teacher anymore.

But the winner . . .

The FBI. Not for spying, not for eavesdropping, not for reading e-mail. For not having e-mail.

The head of the bureau's New York office says that a large number of his 2,000 employees do not have external e-mail accounts, the dot-gov addresses, because "we just don't have the money." You got it. Budget cutbacks. On e-mail addresses.

Your e-mail—they might have. Their own—not so much.

Bean counters at the FBI, *today's Worst Persons in the World!*

Elementary Mistake

MARCH 22, 2006

The bronze: Judge Stanton S. Kaplan of Broward County, Florida. When convicted traffic offender Tank Carter turned himself in to begin his sentence a month late, Carter explained he knew he'd done wrong and was prepared for the judge to increase his six-month jail term, but he'd had a reason. His brother Tyrone had played in the Super Bowl for the Pittsburgh Steelers and he just had to be there. Kaplan reportedly said, "Yeah, right," and increased Tank Carter's sentence from six months to five years for driving without a license. But Tank Carter's brother Tyrone did play in the Super Bowl for the Steelers. And the judge increased his sentence by 10 times.

The runner-up: Christopher Killion of Tulsa. He stopped by a local watering hole and left his 4-year-old son in the car, telling him to stay in it, or "Monsters would eat him." The kid braved the threat and eventually went looking for Dad in the establishment. He found him, inside the . . . strip club. Dad's been arrested.

But the winner:

The makers of Clorox. As part of a direct marketing scheme, they sent boxes of samples of Clorox disinfectant, Clorox gel, and Clorox disinfectant wipes to an elementary school in Golden, Colorado. The school gave the samples out to the kids.

Since the packages of wipes had pictures of little girls on them, some of the kindergartners and first to fifth graders used the disinfectant-laced towels on their own faces. Clorox says the school screwed up. The samples were supposed to be handed out to parents.

The Clorox Company, *today's Worst Persons in the World!*

All in the Family

The bronze: Fidel Castro. The dictator's former go-fer reveals that Castro has his used underwear burned to avoid assassination attempts using laundry chemicals. Which begs the question: when Woody Allen spoofed Castro in the1971 movie *Bananas*, showing a dictator who ordered his people to wear their underwear on the outside from now on, did he know, or was it just a really good guess?

Our runner-up: Phillip Williams of MacDill Air Force Base in Florida. Police say Mr. Williams had just bought some crack cocaine, but wasn't sure he'd gotten the real thing. How do they know this? Because, they say, he went up to two uniformed officers and asked them to test his crack pipe to make sure it was the real thing.

But the winner . . .

Barbara Bush. The former first lady. Mother of the president.

The *Houston Chronicle* reported today, and her chief of staff confirmed, that Mrs. Bush made a generous donation to the Hurricane Katrina Relief Fund, co-chaired by her husband, the former president, and former president Clinton. But there was a catch.

The money she donated had to be spent on buying computer software programs for schools in Houston. Computer software programs for schools in Houston sold by her son, Neil.

You'd think if a woman has reached her 80th birthday, she'd understand that if you make a donation to a charity and then make the charity give the donation to your son, it's not a damned donation any more!

Barbara Bush, *today's Worst Person in the World!*

Don't Pat the Bunny

MARCH 25, 2006

The bronze: To the police in Newport, South Wales. They have shut down a device used by a storeowner trying to break up the gangs of teenagers from hanging out around the storefront. It's called "the Mosquito," and it emits a high-pitched whine, audible to those 20 and under—and not to those over 20. Police said it worked like a charm, but they were worried it might start local dogs barking.

Runner-up: Jacques Chirac, president of France, who stalked out of a European Union summit meeting because of what one of his French colleagues was saying. Well, not exactly what he was saying, but how he was saying it. In English.

The delegate was asking European leaders to "resist national protectionism," but because he wasn't saying it in French, Chirac bolted. Fou!

But the winner . . .

Ellen Greene of Framingham, Massachusetts. Her son came back from the fourth grade with a drawing done by a school counselor. It shows the word "LOVE" with the "O" replaced by a bunny head. The boy didn't know what the bunny had to do with it. Turns out the drawing had been made for a girl who had Playboy logo earrings.

Ms. Greene raised heck at the school, claiming sex was being introduced into the fourth grade, and explained the bunny logo to her son and her other kids. Rather than simply telling them it was just a cute bunny rabbit.

Yes, that's right, she introduced sex into the fourth grade, then blamed the school.

Ellen Greene, *today's Worst Person in the World!*

Church Business
MARCH 30, 2006

The bronze to Supreme Court Justice Antonin Scalia. As he left church last Sunday, he reportedly made an obscene hand gesture to a reporter. But the judge denied there was any gesture until a photo of the incident, shot by a freelance photographer, showed up today in the *Boston Herald*.

Now Justice Scalia "has no comment."

The runner-up: Bill O'Reilly! He's declared the American press the "most damaging institution in the country today, because it's so blatantly partisan and dishonest intellectually."

Well, if that's true, Bill-O, if the American media is now partisan and intellectually dishonest—your work here is done, you've accomplished what you set out to do.

But the winner . . .

A double-Bill! Claiming that the archbishop of Los Angeles, Cardinal Roger Mahony, favors immigration because "he knows he'll get those people in church when he doesn't have anybody in church anymore."

Uh-oh, Bill. That's a Catholic biggy right there. You may be going to hell.

Of course, one could argue you're already in your own private one.

Bill O'Reilly, *today's Worst Person in the World!*

Endurance

The bronze to Fanny Amun, acting secretary general of Nigeria's soccer league. Its referees apparently take a lot of bribes to fix league games. Amun's solution? Take the bribes, then screw over the bribers: "Referees should only pretend to fall for the bait, but make sure the result doesn't favor those offering the bribe."

And your advice to your refs when the fixers feel double-crossed? "Run," perhaps?

The runner-up: David M. Boudreaux, a youth minister in Liberty, Missouri. He's been arrested on assault charges after a dodgeball game with the kids from his church. One of the 16-year-olds managed to hit Boudreaux squarely in the face with the ball, and he reacted poorly, knocking the kid to the ground, then kicking him in the groin.

Hold on. What kind of church lets nearly fully grown kids play dodgeball?

But our winner . . .

Radio's Neal Boortz. Congresswoman Cynthia McKinney was arrested after allegedly striking a police officer at a Capitol Hill security checkpoint. Boortz declared that Representative McKinney, who is an African American, has a new hairstyle that makes her look "like a ghetto slut."

"Like an explosion at a Brillo-pad factory."

"Like Tina Turner peeing on an electric fence."

And like "a shih tzu."

He claims he's permitted to say these things because he's "endured years of 'bald' remarks." OK, endure this one. You're a bald racist.

That's "boor" plus a "tz" . . .

Neal Boortz, *today's Worst Person in the World!*

What are you, Bill, Osama Bin Laden's spokesman?

A Small Problem

APRIL 3, 2006

The bronze to the ever-popular Congresswoman Jean Schmidt of Ohio. Here we go:

Another complaint has been filed against her with the Ohio Board of Elections. Some of her campaign literature said she got two bachelor's degrees from the University of Cincinnati. Turns out she only got one. Her office contends she had enough credits for the second one, only she never bothered to "collect it." Well, who among us hasn't just left a degree unclaimed?

The runner-up: An unnamed suspect in South Bend, Indiana. Police there have tied together two developments. One: a string of thefts in which the only things stolen have been the doors off ovens. Two: a guy selling flat-screen TVs for as little as $300.

You got it. He stuck a cord to the oven doors, bubble-wrapped them, stuck Wal-Mart store labels on them, and waited for the customers' greed to take care of the rest.

But the winners . . .

NBW, the operators of the nuclear power plant at Phillipsburg, in Badden-Wuerttemberg in Germany. They've had a small problem since the 10th of March. They've lost a dozen keys to a nuclear power plant.

German authorities report NBW spent the first week looking for them, then they decided they'd better tell the nuclear regulatory agency, and then they decided to change the 150 locks on the place.

What's German for "Smithers? Did you leave the keys in your other pants?"

NBW, *today's Worst Persons in the World!*

Dewey Defeats Truman

APRIL 4, 2006

The bronze: Shawn Ray Nguyen and Burlie Sholar III, two of our air marshals, keeping the skies safe for us, the passenger public. And for cocaine smugglers. They've pleaded guilty to smuggling cocaine, drug money, and fraudulent government documents past airport security and onto a plane to Las Vegas.

Runner-up: Kelly Johnston. She caught her 15-year-old daughter stealing some of her stuff. The punishment? Punched the girl in the face and in the head and handcuffed her to a bed for 17 hours. All because the daughter had gotten into Mom's marijuana stash.

Ms. Johnston has gotten a 13-month term in county jail, and three years' probation.

But the winners . . .

Amazon.com. The internet mega-store got a head start, pursuing that big NCAA basketball championship merchandise dollar. It sent out an e-mail to an unknown number of its customers yesterday morning with the subject line: "UCLA Wins!" and offered 2006 UCLA National Championship shirts and caps and other overpriced junk.

This was several hours before UCLA lost the national championship game to Florida, 73–57.

***Amazon.com**, today's Worst Persons in the World!*

Ugly, Indeed

APRIL 5, 2006

The bronze: To authorities in Great Britain. They stopped a flight as it was leaving Durham for London, and off it pulled passenger Harraj Mann for questioning. His crime? On the taxi ride to the airport, he had sung along with the "Immigrant Song" by Led Zeppelin and "London Calling" by the Clash. And because of lyrics like "war is declared and battle come down," the cabdriver thought he might be a terrorist.

The runner-up: Brett R. Steidler of Reamstown, Pennsylvania. He's pleaded guilty to building a tiny bomb and mailing it to a cosmetic surgeon because he wasn't satisfied with the job the surgeon had done. Mr. Steidler had gone to him for penis enlargement.

But our winner:

The cheerleaders for the UCLA basketball team, which lost to Florida Monday night in the national championship game. Florida center Joakim Noah says that during the game, the UCLA cheerleaders—the girls, mind you—taunted him and called him "Ugly."

Now it's possible that Noah should be the nominee here because they might have just been spelling out "U-C-L-A" and maybe he heard "U-G-L-Y."

Otherwise . . .

The UCLA Bruin Cheerleaders, *today's Worst Persons in the World!*

Operation Predator

APRIL 5, 2006

How about protecting America's teenagers from sexual predators who happen to be on the Department of Homeland Security payroll?

Brian Doyle, the department's deputy press secretary, is the second agency official to be charged with a sexual offense involving a child since late last year. He is accused of trying to seduce a child into online sex and of transmitting pornographic material, authorities saying that last night when Mr. Doyle thought he was chatting online with a 14-year-old girl, one whom he had been in communication with for three weeks, he was actually talking with an undercover detective who had been posing as the teenager.

Officers moved in to arrest Mr. Doyle in his Maryland home, and officials said that at no point did he ever try to conceal his identity. In fact, he flaunted it, not only allegedly telling the detective posing as the little girl his name and title, but also giving her his office phone number and that of his government-issued cell phone.

Ironically, the arrest came only hours after dramatic hearings on Capitol Hill about Internet predators, where one young man shared the story of how, as a lonely 13-year-old with a Web camera, he was pulled into the world of child pornography. Brian Doyle's boss said today that the department is cooperating fully with the investigation.

As for the other Homeland Security official charged with a sex crime, his name is Frank Figueroa, former head of Operation Predator, the Homeland Security program specifically targeting child sex predators. Mr. Figueroa today pled no contest that he exposed and fondled himself in front of a teenage girl in the food court of a mall in Orlando last October.

Brian Doyle and Frank Figueroa, today's
Honorary Worst Persons in the World!

Know Your Enemy

The bronze to Lynn Lempel and Will Shortz, the creator and editor, respectively, of the crossword puzzle in Monday's *New York Times*. 43 Down. Clue: "Scoundrel," eight letters. Answer: "Scumbag." Creator Lempel said she had no idea that the word originated as slang for a condom.

Actually, slang for a used condom.

The runner-up: Congressman Curt Weldon of Pennsylvania. Complaining that a challenger for his seat, former Navy admiral Joe Sestak, should have sent his daughter to a hospital in Pennsylvania or maybe Delaware for treatment, rather than the one she went to, in Washington. Five-year-old Alexandra Sestak has a malignant brain tumor.

But the winner . . .

I knew he couldn't stop himself. After several days of circumspection, Billo explained on the radio that if Hillary Clinton is elected president: "The first thing bin Laden and his killers are gonna do is say 'Oh yeah, this is good. We like this,' and they'll test her . . ."

What are you, Osama Bin Laden's spokesman? Oh, holy crap, I never thought of that!

Bill O'Reilly, *today's Worst Person in the World!*

Your Other Right Hand

The bronze: To the fans of the Italian soccer team Inter Milan. As supporters worldwide will do, they hastened to the airport to greet their heroes as they came back from a victory on the road at Ascoli. And *attacked* them.

Despite the win, Inter Milan was mathematically eliminated from the league's championship and some fans pelted them with rocks and other debris.

The runner-up: An unidentified motorcycle cop in the San Fernando Valley outside Los Angeles. He gave a jaywalking ticket to a pedestrian who took too long to cross a five-lane-wide street, a street where the duration of the "walk" signal is apparently way too short. The pedestrian, facing a $114 ticket, is 82-year-old Mayvis Coyle.

But the winner . . .

Dr. Mary Ellen Beatty of Tampa. She has been fined $20,000 for operating on the wrong part of a patient's body. Again. Three times now. She's a hand surgeon; in the latest gaffe, she cut the wrong finger.

Remember I mentioned earlier George Carlin's old joke about how there has to be, literally, a worst doctor in the world? And somebody has an appointment to see them tomorrow? Might be this one.

Dr. Mary Ellen Beatty, *today's Worst Person in the World!*

Monkey's Paw

Number three: Mrs. Richard Mellon Scaife. The estranged wife of that guy, you know, Mr. Right-Wing Conspiracy. She's in trouble with the law for the second time in five months, accused of assaulting three of her husband's employees, in a desperate attack to recover her dog, whom hubby had taken from her home the day before.

Heck, why are we making her the nominee? After all, she's been married to Richard Mellon Scaife; it's surprising she only attacked three of his employees.

The runner-up: Brit Hume of Fox News. Hey, wherever you are on the immigration debate, can you abide somebody characterizing yesterday's nationwide, peaceful protests by immigrants the way he did? As a "repellent spectacle"?

Hey, pal, I've seen your newscast. You're skating on thin ice when you call something else a "repellent spectacle."

But the winners . . .

James Snyder and Mary Jo Jensen of Waterloo, Iowa, are under arrest for submitting the obituary of her son to the local newspaper. The 17-year-old boy is not dead, he's not even sick. But they had taken a lot of time off from their jobs at Tyson Foods in Waterloo, telling their bosses that the kid was dying. They are charged with having made up a story about her own son dying to get a couple of days off.

James Snyder and Mary Jo Jensen, *today's*
Worst Persons in the World!

The Leaders and Worst

The bronze: Event planners at the DaVinci Academy in Ogden, Utah. They sent out 500 invitations for the charter school's annual benefit dinner, advertising a special guest appearance by "Jon Stewart of the *Daily Show*." Turns out there was a slight bit of confusion. They'd actually booked Mr. John A. Stewart, former motivational speaker, and part-time professional wrestler from Chicago.

Our runners-up: Sara and Kris Everson of Grain Valley, Missouri. They sent out a letter to neighbors announcing the birth of sextuplets, asking for donations to help raise their six new kids. Problem is, Mrs. Everson wasn't even pregnant. It was a scam. She and hubby have been arrested and are facing fraud charges.

But the winners . . .

Execs at the Wolverine meatpacking company in Detroit, Michigan. They say they warned 15 Mexican immigrant women that if they skipped work to go to an immigration rally, they'd be fired. The women say they got no such warning. Either way, the workers were fired.

Wait a minute: "The Wolverine Packing Company"? Are you guys actually able to make money selling wolverine meat?

The Wolverine Packing Company, *today's*
Worst Persons in the World!

What's in a Name?

APRIL 13, 2006

The bronze to officers and others at the U.S. military base in Bogram in Afghanistan. They've been storing sensitive information on computer flash memory drives. Little stuff, like classified reports, documents marked "Secret," lists of local militants to be killed or captured, the social security numbers of military personnel, etc. How do we know this?

Because the flash memory drives have been popped out of laptops stolen from the Bogram base and are now on sale at the local bazaar, 200 yards away from the base.

The runner-up: Svetlana Yankovsky. Identified as a well-known Russian Gypsy singer and dancer, unfortunately for the other passengers aboard a flight from Vegas to New York, she's also a well-known lush. She was drinking wine out of a bottle as the plane taxied in Vegas. When the crew told her to stop, she began chanting, hexing the plane, predicting it would crash, and declaring that all the passengers, their children, and grandchildren would die. They put down in Denver, where Ms. Yankovsky was arrested.

If she was that good at seeing the future, how in the hell did she miss that little detail, huh?

But the winner . . .

The folks at the Transportation Security Administration who supervise the no-fly list, the one that keeps all the guys named David Nelson and Peter Williams grounded because somebody somewhere thinks there's a terrorist using that name, or a similar one. This time the list kept Daniel Brown from boarding his flight from L.A. to Minneapolis.

Staff Sergeant Daniel Brown, going home to Minneapolis after eight months' service with the Marines in Iraq.

The TSA No-Fly List Guru, *today's*
Worst Person in the World!

Multiplicity

And we have a hat trick.

The bronze: Ann Coulter for explaining that the immigration problem could be resolved thusly: "I'd build a wall. In fact, I'd hire illegal immigrants to build the wall. And throw out the illegals who are here." You did read "The Cask of Amontillado," didn't you, Ann?

The runner-up: Comedian Rush Limbaugh. After Ben Domenech resigned from the *Washington Post*'s new conservative "Red America" blog, admitting plagiarism as he did so, Limbaugh explained that the *Post* had simply "buckled" to the left and "concocted some phony excuse that the guy that they had hired was a plagiarist." I wish Rush would plagiarize a good idea from somebody.

But the winner . . .

Billo! After a newspaper editorial chastised talk-show hosts railing against an "attack on Easter," last night O'Reilly dismissed the piece as a "nutty diatribe" and reassured everybody, "there is no attack on Easter."
This just two days after he had talked about how Christmas and Easter have "been attacked by secular interests." And one day before, according to his Web site, he'll do a segment titled "Easter Under Siege." There isn't, there is, there is.
Maybe there are multiple Bill O'Reillys. Run for your lives!

Bill O'Reilly, *today's Worst Person in the World!*

Looks Bad and Smells Worse

APRIL 17, 2006

The bronze: Vince McMahon of World Wrestling Entertainment. The man who somehow actually worsened the reputation of pro wrestling has done it again, claiming that a week from Sunday his organization will televise a tag-team match featuring McMahon and his son Shane, versus Shawn Michaels and . . . God. Yes, the Almighty.

How to save time by blaspheming in all the religions all at once.

The runner-up is Angie Marquez, principal of an elementary school in Inglewood, California. Trying to prevent her students from walking out of classes during last week's immigration protests—which she had the right to do—she got a little "overzealous." She imposed a full lockdown, meaning kids couldn't leave their classrooms even to use the bathroom. That's right: they had to use buckets.

But the winner . . .

Michelle Malkin. Military recruiters showed up at an on-campus job fair at the University of California at Santa Cruz, which was their right. Four students showed up and protested their presence, which was *their* right. Malkin blogged about it, which was *her* right.

But she also posted the names and home phone numbers of the protesting students, who as a result have been inundated with death threats. And she will not take the phone numbers down from her blog. And if she thinks that is also her right, then she's even crazier and dumber than we all thought.

Michelle Malkin, *today's Worst Person in the World!*

Garbage

The bronze to the Arkansas Teacher Retirement System. It sent its 50,000 members a brochure on estate planning, complete with a toll-free number. As part of the epidemic in this country of misprinted toll-free phone numbers, the number actually connected the retired teachers to a foot fetish phone line.

Well, it is one way to spend your estate.

Our runner-up: Steve Forbes. The publisher and former presidential wannabe explained to Fox News over the weekend that "when we have the confrontation" with Iran, the good news is that "the price of oil will drop, probably around 15 dollars a barrel."

Chaos? Tension? War? Just so long as gas prices drop.

But the winner . . .

Kimberly Williamson Butler, the candidate for mayor of New Orleans who had on her Web site a photo of herself not in New Orleans but at the French Quarter exhibit at Disneyland. The giveaway was the Disneyland garbage can near the center of the image. So she's changed the photo.

To a new photo of her in New Orleans? No, the same one—only without the Disneyland garbage can. Because lawyers at Disney said they were looking into the situation!

Kimberly Williamson Butler, *today's*
Worst Person in the World!

A Losing Bet

The bronze: Robert Sillerman. Already the owner of *American Idol*, he could be in a position now to put an entire industry out of work. He's bought 85 percent of Elvis Presley Enterprises, which controls the King's name and likeness. He's going to open an interactive Elvis exhibit and cabaret show in Vegas, and says, "If we were going to do a show that was based on Elvis impersonators, then obviously it wouldn't make sense to have unauthorized Elvis impersonators." Thirty thousand unlicensed Elvis impersonators are thus not saying "Thank you; thank you very much."

Runner-up: The good old Department of Homeland Security. It's just awarded a $385 million contract to the Halliburton subsidiary KBR to provide "temporary detention and processing capabilities" here in the USA. It's a plan to prepare for, on American soil, "an emergency influx of immigrants, or to support the rapid development of new programs" in the event of other emergencies, such as "a natural disaster." Concentration camps, right? Am I reading that wrong? Immigrants . . . new programs . . . temporary detention capabilities . . .

But the winner . . .

The National Scold, Bill Bennett. Reacting to the Pulitzer Prizes—the one Dana Priest got for the secret CIA gulags in Europe and those James Risen and Eric Lichtblau of the *New York Times* got for exposing the NSA domestic spying—Mr. Bennett says they shouldn't have gotten Pulitzers. They should've gotten jail time. Now, Bill, no need to get catty.

We know you're just upset because you didn't bet on the Priest/Risen/Lichtblau trifecta in any of the Pulitzer wagering books in Vegas.

Bill Bennett, *today's Worst Person in the World!*

Go Ahead, Jeff

APRIL 19, 2006

We soon won't have Scott McClellan to kick around anymore, giving us just a brief window of opportunity to keep kicking Scott McClellan around. As press secretaries go, he has been as loquacious as he has been opaque. Never before has a political flak used so many words to say so very little:

"Yes, this is getting into where someone engaged in a blame game. And I'm just not going to engage in the blame game. What you're doing is trying to engage in a game of finger pointing, the blame game."

"Well, I think we all know that once it is made public, then it's going to be news, and we'll let those—the legal process proceed in those instances. The president's view is that we need to let the legal process work. That's what the legal process will proceed to address. We need to let the legal process proceed, and that's what the president believes. This is a different circumstance, and we're going to let the legal process, we're going to let the legal process work. . . . We're going to let the legal process work."

"We are fighting them there so that we don't have to fight them here. September 11 taught us . . ."

"Go ahead, Jeff."

"Go ahead, Jeff."

"Go ahead, Jeff."

"I'm glad, I'm glad you brought that up, Jeff."

"Jeff, go ahead."

"I'm not even going to dignify that with a response. Go ahead, Jeff."

"I spoke with them so that I could come back to you and say that they were not involved."

"This is a question relating to an ongoing investigation."

"Again, you're continuing to ask questions relating to an ongoing criminal investigation."

"Again, these are all questions coming up in the context of an ongoing criminal investigation."

"I'm simply not going to comment on an ongoing investigation."

"This continues to be an ongoing criminal investigation."

"Again, you're asking questions relating to an ongoing investigation, and I think I . . ."

"Do you have questions on another topic?"

"I think you all in this room know me very well, and you know the type of person that I am. You and many others in this room have dealt with me for quite some time, and I'm someone who believes in dealing in a very straightforward way with you all as well, and that's what I've worked to do."

What's next for Scott McClellan? That's an ongoing personnel matter. We can't comment on that except to name . . .

Scott McClellan *today's Honorary Worst Person in the World!*

Hoochie-Coochie Plan

APRIL 20, 2006

The bronze: Jo Ann Emerson, congresswoman from southeastern Missouri. She responded to a letter from a constituent, with a closing paragraph that read, "Please feel free to contact me with other matters that are of importance to you. I am honored to serve as your Representative in the U.S. Congress. I think you are a [bleep.]" Congresswoman Emerson seems to be blaming that last line on a member of her staff.

Problem is, she not only personally signed the letter, she hand-wrote the P.S., "Please forgive the delay in responding."

Our runner-up: Barry Bonds, fined five thousand bucks by major league baseball. No, not for steroids. Not for fake crying on TV. For using improperly designed wristbands. Bonds doesn't wear headbands, because, of course, they don't make them big enough to fit around his giant balloonish noggin.

But the winner . . .

Lidia Alvarado, a 44-year-old woman accused of trying to smuggle marijuana and a grenade into a prison in El Salvador. Accused of hiding them in her . . . where-babies-come-from. No idea if she was caught by bomb-sniffing dogs or because she was walking funny. A Salvadoran official says they're now heightening security at all prisons because the discovery showed that "the inmates are planning something."

Yeah—like a talent show!

***Lidia Alvarado**, today's Worst Person in the World!*

Upon Further Examination

APRIL 20, 2006

She began to doubt it, says one of his victims, not when he sidled up to her when she was taking out the garbage, not when he explained it was a free service of the community, not when he pulled a stethoscope out of an old black nurse's bag, not even when he told her that for the full benefits of what he was offering, she needed to take off her clothes and lie on a bed and her boyfriend had to leave the room. Her doubts that the city of Lauderdale Lakes had hired 76-year-old Philip Winikoff as a door-to-door breast examiner occurred only when he failed to put on surgical gloves as he began to examine her as she lay there naked in her apartment. Not one, but two women actually fell for this guy's routine, say police, in—and it can only *be* in—*Countdown*'s official state, Florida. The alleged perpetrator, Mr. Winikoff, allegedly told a 35-year-old woman in an apartment complex there that he was a doctor from North Miami Hospital offering free door-to-door breast examinations. He carried a medical bag, his soon-to-be victim had her boyfriend translate, and then she allowed him to perform the exam on her on the couch in her home while her boyfriend watched.

It was later in the bedroom when she was naked and he didn't go for the surgical gloves that the victim determined he was not a doctor, and then he fled as she yelled. Police said they found him conning a second woman, a 33-year-old, a block away. He was arrested on charges of sexual battery and simple assault. Authorities believe there may be additional victims. And by the way, the old medical bag he carried was his wife's. She is a registered nurse.

Philip Winikoff, today's Honorary Worst Person in the World!

Clowns

The bronze to Bill O'Reilly. Yes, he's slipping, but he still occasionally gets off a good one. Whining about measures in California preventing arrests of the homeless, he said, "The ACLU wants to force society to house people who will not support themselves, who will not do it, because they want to get drunk, or they want to get high, or they want—they don't want to work, they're too lazy."

Can we get him a calendar? It's 2006. The idea that all the homeless are there by choice vanished about 1976.

Our runner-up: Michael Thelemann of Bray, Oklahoma. He's 45, he's unmarried, so he put up a sign in his yard offering a thousand dollars for "Miss Right." The community is aghast. "What's the problem?" Mr. Thelemann asks. "I'm just somebody who is getting up there in years, and I'm looking for a born-again, God-fearing virgin between the ages of 12 and 24 who can bear me children." Might want to shift that age window a tad north, buddy . . .

But the winner . . .

The fire department of Des Moines, Iowa. The *Washington Times* reported that the department took their assistance to firefighters counterterrorism grant from Homeland Security and spent $69,000 on puppets and clowns.

No, no, not kickbacks to Michael Chertoff. Actual puppets and clowns to a group that teaches fire safety through puppet and clown shows.

For keeping Iowa safe from terrorism using puppets and clowns . . .

The fire department of Des Moines, *today's*
Worst Persons in the World!

I Scream

The bronze goes to—Bill, you're just not trying anymore, are you? He says now that about Iraq and the generals criticism of Don Rumsfeld, "I have to go on what my military analysts, people paid by Fox News, say to me. I can't base my opinion on anything else."

Like the guy, Colonel Hunt, who mocked the idea that there weren't enough armored vehicles in Iraq. Or Oliver North, who said Saddam Hussein would be killed within three days of any invasion by his own people. Or Colonel McGinnis, who said that the reality is we're not going to see thousands of American deaths. Those guys? Those geniuses.

The runner-up, and this hurts, is one of my friends, Keith Hernandez, the New York Mets baseball announcer and former first baseman, who should be in the Baseball Hall of Fame. He saw a woman in the dugout of the San Diego Padres during the game yesterday and said, on the air, "I won't say women belong in the kitchen, but they don't belong in the dugout. I think this is a man's game, and I feel strongly about it." She was one of the Padres team trainers.

You'd think differently about that, Keith, if your back went out suddenly.

But the winner . . .

Ben and Jerry's ice cream. They have evidently run out of flavor names that are both creative and not controversial. The newest flavor, based on an ale and stout drink, is "black and tan." The Irish, Irish-Americans, and even many in England are horrified.

The Black and Tan's were the extralegal military police recruited by the British in Ireland as the troubles came to the fore in the 1920s. What's next: Brownshirt flavor ice cream or Gestapo crunch? You get the idea.

Ben and Jerry's ice cream, *today's*
Worst Persons in the World!

The Word Could Have Been Love

APRIL 25, 2006

The bronze goes to a company in Tibet now marketing a cigarette that, it says, does not stain teeth and replaces all the vitamins that smoking sucks out of you. It's called Vitacig. Roger Ouellette says he's a nonsmoker, but he invented these for his wife, Gisele, who has smoked since she was 14. She says, "I am happy because I don't have to quit anymore." Gisele, your husband is trying to kill you.

The runner up: Amy Duckworth, arrested on charges of trying to sneak cocaine in to her husband in the jail in Huntington, Indiana, inside a pair of bibles. Nice touch.

But the winner . . .

Psychic Joe Power, appearing on a British pay-per-view televised seance designed to contact John Lennon. His mike suddenly went dead, and a voice from beyond the grave could be heard. It was John Lennon saying, "Peace. The message is peace."

Wow. You got John Lennon to say "Peace"? Who'd have ever thought he'd have said "Peace"! Of all the words, that's going way out on a limb!

Joe Power, *unimaginative psychic, today's Worst Person in the World!*

Rerun

The bronze to Dusten Williams of Beaverton, Oregon. His face was made up in an apparent salute to *Revenge of the Sith* while, police say, he was threatening kids outside a school with a fake handgun.

Our runners-up: Minneapolis police officers Steven Herron and Lindsay Anderson—no, not the British filmmaker. They are under arrest in Columbia Heights, Minnesota. First, Ms. Anderson allegedly drunk-drove her car into a parked car, and when the Columbia Heights cops wouldn't let her walk away, she swore at them and flipped the bird. Whereupon Mr. Herron, her fiancé— and also a policeman—was difficult enough that the Columbia Heights cops had to taser him.

But our winner . . .

Oh, that's better. Billo's coming to a boil again. His latest mortal enemy: the newspaper the *Syracuse Post-Standard*, which wrote about him . . . blah blah blah . . . we get it . . .

He's inducted them into the new Bill O'Reilly Hall of Shame. The *Countdown* Hall of Fame would sue, but, heck, if anybody's an expert on shame, it's Bill—so we'll let this pass.

But he also says, "Beginning *today*, the smear stops here." You're going to stop smearing people? How you gonna fill an hour every night, Bill? Reruns of *The Jetsons*?

Bill O'Reilly, *today's Worst Person in the World!*

Horseshoes and Hand Grenades

APRIL 28, 2006

You'll recognize the theme quickly.

The bronze goes to the fire department of Lemont, Illinois. High school student Rebecca George volunteered for one of the department's safety demonstrations. She played "Injured Student Number One." She has sued because, she says, while she was lying there pretending to be injured, firefighters tried to really injure her, by kicking her and stepping on her.

The silver goes to the St. Petersburg police department. They, too, were staging a drill, a training exercise in which an officer pretending to be a golf-club-wielding passerby was to be arrested. But two officers who didn't know it was a drill reportedly happened on the scene and promptly tasered the officer pretending to be the wielder.

But the winner . . .

Counterterror officials at the airport in Belgrade in Serbia-Montenegro. They put actual bombs in about five pieces of luggage being passed through the airport screening system, and their crack bomb-sniffing dogs found four of them. Four out of five.

The other bomb, fortunately without any detonation device, was apparently shipped in the cargo hold of a plane bound for London.

Counterterror officials at the Belgrade Airport, *today's Worst Persons in the World!*

Plea Bargain
APRIL 28

There's a plea deal, there's a rehab program, and there will be one charge of doctor-shopping that will remain pending against Limbaugh until about November 1 of 2007. And whatever else happens or does not, there will ever, forever be Rush Limbaugh, the mug shot. Rush behind bars.

After three years of jousting with prosecutors in the Palm Beach area over accusations of doctor-shopping and pill-popping, of getting new prescriptions for painkillers like oxycontin from physician after physician, of possessing literally thousands of pills, and using his own household staff to collect them in some cases, Limbaugh turned himself in at about 4:00 P.M. eastern time today.

The process, the mug shot, the bail of $3,000 were over in about an hour, with the formal filing of the negotiated resolution to come sometime during the day Monday. Limbaugh entered a not-guilty plea to the remaining charge of fraud to conceal information to obtain prescriptions. It will remain open for 18 months. If he continues with the rehab program for drug users and avoids any other legal problems, that charge will be dropped. He's also agreed to pay $30,000 to help—to the state to help defray the costs of its investigation.

*Rush Limbaugh, jailbird, today's
Honorary Worst Person in the World!*

Does that opinion come
with the sheet and
the hood, Bill?

Now and Forever

MAY 1, 2006

The bronze goes to the Cablevision company, serving Yonkers, New York. It hit a 62-year-old retired schoolteacher with a bill for $1,431 for pay-per-view porn and gangsta-rap specials. It says that if she didn't order it, somebody else in her house did. She points out that her only regular visitor is her 81-year-old mother, and, "I don't think she wants to watch porn."

Runners-up: Ronald Arnold and Ryan Dawson of Wilsonville, Missouri, accused by prosecutors there of force-feeding a bowl of vodka to an 8-week-old puppy. The dog has recovered.

But our winner . . .

Billo. Announcing that there is a "very powerful far-left cabal . . . and these guys have made inroads, inroads particularly at NBC News." Oh, here we go.

He also insisted Fox News is not a "right-wing enterprise," then declared his conviction that he also believes in brownies and elves.

Now and forever . . .

Bill O'Reilly, *today's Worst Person in the World!*

Tortured Logic

The bronze goes to 17-year-old Jake Sullivan of Dover, New Hampshire. He got a fake ID and tried to buy beer. The name on the ID, unfortunately for Jake, was that of the principal at his own school.

The runner-up: Tim Tompkins, president of New York City's Times Square Alliance. He knows exactly what midtown Manhattan needs: a permanent glass staircase to nowhere in Duffy Square at 47th Street. Sixteen feet high. Heated in the winter. Room for a thousand tourists to sit on. And you're going to do what with the homeless people who want to sleep there?

But our winner . . .

Laura Ingraham. Having already reached the dubious conclusion that "the mainstream media" is "supporting" amnesty for illegal immigrants, she offered this tortured logic as support: "NBC, ABC, and CBS, throw in CNN and MSNBC, they think these are, you know, new viewers, new listeners, new customers to the more liberal viewpoint . . ."

Uh huh. And the fact that at least many of these folks seem to prefer hearing and seeing the news in their native languages—how did you rationalize that again?

Laura Ingraham, *today's Worst Person in the World!*

Good Morning, Mr. Phelps

MAY 2, 2006

Promotion people of all stripes will tell you the best kind of publicity stunt is "explosive." The problem comes when it explodes but in your face. Tom Cruise and Paramount Pictures experienced just that, both for their new movie *Mission Impossible III* and for Cruise's career.

To promote the movie, Paramount made a deal with the *Los Angeles Times*. Forty-five hundred *Times* newspaper vending boxes around southern California were rigged with a special device. It played the *Mission Impossible* theme whenever somebody put in their coins and pulled out a paper. What could possibly go wrong?

How about the fact that the automatic music-playing machine was a six-inch-long, two-inch-wide red plastic box with wires sticking out of it, easily visible to newspaper purchasers—you know, like a pipe bomb.

The first time somebody called the police in the city of Santa Clarita, nobody knew about the promotional scheme, so the cops got the bomb squad, and the *L.A. Times* newspaper box got blowed up real good. Presumably to the musical accompaniment of the theme from *Mission Impossible*. Subsequent calls about the so-called singing newsracks have been met by police reassurance.

***Tom Cruise and Paramount Pictures**, today's Honorary Worst Persons in the World!*

Marriage Counselor

MAY 3, 2006

There's a theme to these: Families.

The bronze to Mayor James Fladung of Ault, Colorado. The Mayor is in jail, arrested after his blood alcohol reached at least .04 percent, which is in the lighter-fluid range. He's also charged with domestic violence and child abuse. His wife and kids are denying those charges. But they won't bail him out, hoping he'll dry out.

Our runner-up: Mrs. Kyle McConnell of Roseville, Michigan. Well, Mrs. Kyle McConnell Battaglia Rice. Those are the names of the three men to whom she is currently married. Police believe there may be another dozen exes, all of whom she has swindled.

But the winner:

Dan Blair, marriage counselor, in suburban Chicago—and Monty Python sketch come to life. His former client Scott Buelow has sued him. Mr. and Mrs. Buelow went to Blair for help. And clearly Mrs. Buelow got some. Mr. Buelow says marriage counselor Blair had an affair with his wife.

Dan Blair, *today's Worst Person in the World!*

By the Numbers

The bronze to passengers and the driver of a trolley in Milan in Italy. Some older women on board pointed out what they thought was an unattended bag. And worse, they said, it seemed to be moving. As the driver prepared to alert the police, another passenger said it was his bag and of course it was moving.

It was filled with four puppies.

Our runner-up: Mayor Frank Melton of Jackson, Mississippi. He's being investigated because last week, driving along a busy interstate, he spotted four buses carrying high school students, and he motioned for the drivers to pull over so he could board the buses and shake hands with, and hug, the kids. "It's been such a stressful two weeks. I wanted to shake their hands. I wanted to touch them. That's all it was."

But our winner:

Pat Patton, programming director of independent San Francisco TV station KRON. Slumped in the ratings, losing money by the barrel, Mr. Patton came up with a solution. Hire an astrologer, a numerologist who told them that KRON's problem was its address.

So they changed it, from 1001 Van Ness Avenue to 1,001,522 Van Ness Avenue. Change a TV operation's fortunes through an astrologer. That's the dopiest management decision—hold on. I've been in TV 25 years now. Actually, compared to most TV management, this guy is relatively logical.

Nevertheless . . .

Pat Patton, *today's Worst Person in the World!*

Sign of the Apocalypse

MAY 5, 2006

The bronze: David Morris, one of the directors of the British soccer team Queens Park Rangers, or QPR. He's been accused of forcing one of his fellow directors to quit. He hired a bunch of thugs to take him into a room and threaten him with a gun until he wrote out his letter of resignation.

The runner-up: Prince Henrik, the father-in-law of Princess Mary of Denmark. Prince Henrik is honorary president of the Danish Dachshund Club and is a noted dog lover, and now we know why. He's told a Danish magazine that he loved eating dogs. That they tasted like rabbit or veal. Well, Prince Henrik is a Great Dane.

But today's winner . . .

Billo! His latest sign of the apocalypse—the one going on in his own head—how New York City schoolteachers have been "instructed" not to do anything even if a 6-year-old says "F-you, you mother-F'er," in school.

Actually, New York City schools discipline code calls language like that a "Level 2 Infraction," which requires at least a conference and perhaps a suspension.

Maybe the teachers have just been told to look the other way if a 6-year-old says "F-you, you mother-F'er" to Bill.

Bill O'Reilly, *today's Worst Person in the World!*

The Wrong Man

MAY 8, 2006

The bronze goes to Senator Bill Frist of Tennessee. He put a secret amendment into a defense bill that shields manufacturers of vaccines from lawsuits claiming negligence or recklessness—you know, like if the vaccine hasn't been tested enough and, say, it kills you. Turns out the amendment was composed for Senator Frist by a trade group for vaccine manufacturers.

The runner-up: Michelle Malkin's back. Complaining about the Texas Rangers baseball team celebrating Cinquo de Mayo by wearing uniforms that read "Los Rangers," she wrote of the selective political correctness: "Can you imagine if someone proposed changing the Rangers' jerseys to 'Confederate Rangers' to celebrate Confederate Heroes' Day?'"

Well, apart from the little sticking point that the confederacy was pro-slavery and in revolt against the legitimate government of the United States, Confederate Heroes' Day is celebrated on January 19, about a month before baseball spring training even begins. Nitwit.

But our winner . . .

Somebody at the U.S. Army recruiting station for the southeast district of Portland, Oregon, whoever it was who signed up 18-year-old Jared Guinther. Nothing against him wanting to sign up; ordinarily that's his right. Nothing against them recruiting him; ordinarily that's their right. Nothing against them signing him; ordinarily that's *their* right.

Except they signed up Jared Guinther and are sending him to basic training in August even though he's autistic.

Somebody at the U.S. Army recruiting station in southeast Portland, Oregon, *today's Worst Person in the World!*

You're an Unprincipled Young Man, Hud.

MAY 9, 2006

The bronze to the Budapest bureau of the news agency Reuters. And an "I told you so." Last week, we reported the saga of two home remodelers who came across an abandoned barrel of rum in a house, drank it, and then discovered at its bottom the pickled remains of the house owner. I had my doubts. Reuters has now withdrawn the story. Police in Budapest told them it happened a decade ago.

The runner-up: Sports columnist Joe Henderson of the *Tampa Tribune*. Picking up the gauntlet of back-filling in defense of Barry Bonds, he writes, as Bonds approaches Ruth's total of 714 home runs, that Ruth "was also illegally juiced . . . Babe's juice was barley-colored and had a foamy head, and it was also against the law to consume it." Henderson suggested that Ruth's total should get an asterisk.

OK, let go over that 18th Amendment, the one that started prohibition, again: "The manufacture, sale, or transportation of intoxicating liquors, the importation thereof into, or the exportation thereof . . . is hereby prohibited." Nothing about drinking. For the last time, during prohibition it wasn't illegal to drink.

But the winner . . .

Alphonso Jackson, the Bush Administration's secretary of housing and urban development. He has told a Dallas real estate forum that he awarded a contract to a bidder, who then came in to thank him. The bidder revealed, "I don't like President Bush." Secretary Jackson says he then canceled the contract.

While prosecutors try to decide if Secretary Jackson broke the law by canceling an already awarded government contract because of the bidder's personal political beliefs, the *Dallas Business Journal* quoted a government contracts consultant, whose reaction pretty much summed it up: "Oh my goodness gracious."

Secretary Alphonso Jackson, *today's*
Worst Person in the World!

Loose Bonding

The bronze, in an update to yesterday's Worst, Dustee Tucker, spokesperson for HUD secretary Alphonso Jackson. To a Dallas newspaper she first repeated her contention that the story Secretary Jackson told of revoking a government contract after the bidder had criticized the president was true. Later in the same day, she said it was a metaphor, that it never really happened.

The department says Ms. Tucker is now on "leave."

Runners-up: Harry Lee Keek and Bradley William Parham, two seniors at Lakeside High School in Hot Springs, Arkansas. They're accused of trying to pay back a teacher they didn't like by mixing laxatives with his tea. Two teachers wound up drinking it and suffered from severe cramps.

But our winners make Harry and Bradley look like pikers.

Julie Hunt of New Portland, Maine. She and her daughter decided to make cookies for one of the daughter's teachers. Mom taught her daughter how to crush the box full of laxatives into the cookie batter. The teacher, of course, shared the cookies with the class, and four seventh and eighth graders got sick. Mom's been charged.

The excuse that it was a nice mother-daughter bonding moment apparently proved unconvincing to police.

Julie Hunt, *today's Worst Person in the World!*

He Had a Friend
MAY 11, 2006

The bronze: Michael Cohn, a Los Angeles psychologist, and Alfred Rava, his attorney. They are suing the baseball team the Los Angeles Angels because in a Mother's Day promotion last year, the Angels gave out special totebags to women 18 and over, but not to him. Cohn is claiming discrimination, asking damages of $4,000 to each man who went to the game last year.

But there's a part two. The attorney, Mr. Rava, seems to have made a hobby of this. He's been part of at least 37 lawsuits since 2003, most of them claiming discrimination because of "ladies' nights" at bars, or discounted tickets to theaters for women or people under 30.

The runner-up: The owners of the venerable British soccer team Arsenal and the stadium at which it has played for nearly a century, Highbury. As it moves to a new stadium, Arsenal had been selling off the seats from the old one until it was discovered that the paint on those seats contained traces of cadmium, a toxic metal that can reduce men's fertility.

But the winner . . .

Radio commentator Neal Boortz, who said that offering counseling to kids traumatized by shootings in schools was just an attempt to sell them on the idea that the government is "responsible for everything." He said there shouldn't have been counseling offered to the students at Columbine.

"I had a friend," Boortz said, "that died of leukemia. Never once did they run a bunch of damn counselors into the school the next day to assist me in getting my feelings out about this issue."

Yeah, Neal, and look how good you turned out.

Neal Boortz, *today's Worst Person in the World!*

It's a Miracle

The bronze: To John Gibson of Fox News Channel. He has now encouraged his viewers to "do your duty, make more babies," because Hispanics are "having more kids than others . . . you know what that means? Twenty-five years and the majority of the population is Hispanic."

John would've placed higher, but it's become obvious he no longer hears what he's saying, and besides which, the average age of his viewers is about 70, so this is only hypothetical eugenics.

Our runner-up: James Frey. First the *Million Little Pieces* fabrication scandal. Now his revelation that the sequel, *My Friend Leonard*, not only also includes fiction in what was sold as a memoir, but the opening scene is fiction.

But the winner . . .

Laura Lee Medley of Los Angeles. She's sued at least four California municipalities, claiming she was injured trying to negotiate her wheelchair through their jurisdictions. Police arrested her on fraud charges in Las Vegas. When they left her alone, for a moment, in her wheelchair, in the hospital, she got up and ran away.

It's a miracle. I have legs! I can see!

***Laura Lee Medley**, today's Worst Person in the World!*

Doomed to Repeat It

The bronze, to the police in Orlando, who appear to have over-reacted just a tad to a senior prank at Edgewater High School. After the officer sent to monitor the traditional event called for backup, the department sent a heavily armed patrol, with helicopters, and arrested and handcuffed five of the thirty or so seniors, who were armed with shaving cream, toilet paper, and Hershey's Syrup.

But the kids were *brandishing* the toilet paper.

The silver, from the "I know where you were coming from, but . . ." file: Michael Maxwell, a teacher at a high school in St. Joseph, Missouri. He gave his seniors a creative writing essay: "Who would you kill and how would you do it?"

But the winner . . .

Oh, Billo. Not only did he compare Al Franken, and some people on the internet and cable television—guess who—to "assassins," but worse, he's rewritten history: "When he [Franken] attacked me . . . a couple of years ago," Billo said, "News Corporation made a mistake in actually trying to sue the guy . . ."

Ummm, Bill, who made the mistake in suing? The one big enough that the judge literally laughed out loud?

Bill O'Reilly, *today's Worst Person in the World!*

Barter System

MAY 16, 2006

The bronze is shared by Mark Yost of *American Spectator* and David Asman of Fox News. Asman concludes that the "heart and mind" of a lot of the journalists covering Iraq "isn't in the war" and therefore "they're not going to report a lot of heroism."

To which Yost says, "a lot of times people are reluctant, they're somewhat embarrassed by people or feel lesser of themselves by people who do incredibly heroic things . . ." so they don't report heroism.

Yeah, boys, that's why the media covered up all the heroism on Flight 93.

The runner-up this time: Consumers Energy of Flint, Michigan. Customer Jacqueline Williams owed the utility $1,662.08. She had to scrounge to pay it, and she should've paid it sooner. And when she got to the office, she found she was a penny short.

The bill's 1662-oh-eight. She's got 1662-oh-seven. So they cut off her electricity for seven hours.

But the winner . . .

Well, we have flip sides of the same issue here. Mayor Troy Anderson of Waldron, Arkansas, accused of patronizing a prostitute, paying for sex, partly in cash, and partly by giving her a discount on her city water bill.

Hey, Baby, how'd you like to have me read your meter?

Mayor Troy Anderson, *today's Worst Person in the World!*

The End Is Near

MAY 17, 2006

The bronze goes to Mrs. Howard Randall of Philadelphia, arrested after she sent her allegedly cheating husband to the hospital, with just a little squeeze. "While he slept," reads the Associated Press report, "police say the woman grabbed and squeezed a part of his male anatomy."

Bonus points: the Philly neighborhood in which the Randalls have lived in wedded bliss is called Nicetown.

Runner-up: City Commissioner Johnny Winton of Miami. Upset at delays in his flight to Houston, he worried ticket agents enough that they called the cops. When they arrived, he told them who he was and what his job was, and suggested they do something that is anatomically impossible. Then he threw a shoulder into one officer's jaw and kicked another in the groin.

Your tax dollars in action.

But the winner . . .

Oh, the psychological end is near. Billo is saying that the *New York Times* and "many far-left thinkers believe the white power structure that controls America is bad, so a drastic change is needed."

Hold on. Bill? You're saying there is a "white power structure that controls America," and you're defending it? Does that opinion come with the sheet and the hood, or do you have to buy those separately?

Bill O'Reilly, *now and forever, today's*
Worst Person in the World!

Tortured Logic Redux

MAY 18, 2006

The bronze goes to the penal and legal system of Lebanon. It has released Hussein Hariri after 17 years in prison for his part in the hijacking of an Air Afrique flight in 1987. He now intends to pursue a new hobby. He's built his own airplane and intends to fly it.

Oh, what could possibly go wrong with this?

The runner-up: Commentator Morton Kondracke, on Fox, blasting Qwest for not cooperating with the NSA phone records sweep that everybody else says never happened: " . . . for a company to opt out and say 'no no no, we're too privacy minded for this'—you know, it's basically helping terrorists."

No, Mort, undermining our freedoms and making money off fear-mongering—that's helping terrorists.

But our winner . . .

I'm telling you—somebody must be his friend, get an intervention. Listen to this tortured logic from Billo, who says his makeup artist was mugged on the streets of New York the other day. "Now," he says, "who does that? Drug addicts desperate for money . . . nine out of 10 of these guys are drug addicts. . . . So, she is a victim of the Mexican drug corruption. And—and—and all you have to do is multiply that by 10 million and you see how all of this corruption in Mexico has infected our society."

The makeup artist was mugged, therefore the mugger was a drug addict, therefore the addiction is Mexico's fault, therefore . . . Ya lost me.

I'm surprised he didn't tie the mugging back somehow to me.

Bill O'Reilly, *still today's Worst Person in the World!*

Bouffon

The bronze: A follow-up to one from last week. We nominated Consumers Energy of Flint, Michigan, for shutting off a woman's electricity for seven hours. She'd been charged $1,662.08. She paid $1,662.07.

A Consumers Energy spokesman told a local newspaper that this was totally inaccurate because "Ironically, the media coverage of this event has overlooked the fact that this customer only had to pay a penny to take care of this bill."

Yeah, after you made her search for it in the dark for seven hours.

The runner-up: Matt Drudge. First-time nominee, long-time schmuck. He posted this at the Drudge Report Web site: Al "Gore and entourage took five cars to travel the 500 yards from hotel to screening of global warming pic in Cannes . . ." Actually, they walked.

Yeah, like it's the first time Drudge just made stuff up.

But—speaking of which—the winner . . .

He's on quite a run. You may remember when he claimed that his boycott of France had cost the French economy "billions of dollars" and quoted as his source the "Paris Business Review," even though there isn't any "Paris Business Review."

Well, now it's Mexico. He's threatening it with O'Reilly Double Secret Probation. If Mexico files one lawsuit over the National Guard troops assigned to the border, Billo says, "I will call for a total boycott of Mexican goods and no travel to your country . . . and if . . . you think it doesn't matter, Mr. Secretary, why don't you give the French ambassador a call? He'll fill you in."

"Allo, m'sieu Ambassador."

"O'Reilly? Mais oui, it's the delusion of grandeur."

*"**M. O'Reilly** is, how you say, today's Worst Person in the World!"*

What Would Jesus Press?

MAY 23, 2006

The bronze goes to our pals at Fox News. The latest bug up their anchor chair: the Al Gore global warming movie. Their captioned question? "Al Gore's Global Warming Movie: Could It Destroy Our Economy?" Seriously.

Did they turn off the oxygen in the newsroom over there?

The runner-up: Wow, Matt Drudge. A full year, never on it, makes it two lists in a row. His Web site had a link, as a news headline, with the teaser "Bonds: I won't stop until I hit 868." The story it links to says Barry Bonds not only wants to beat Hank Aaron's North American home run record of 755, but also Sadaharu Oh's world home run record of 868. The site to which Drudge attributed it: "WTF, TV."

WTF. Now what could that possibly stand for?

But the winner . . .

Pat Robertson. He is now selling Fitness Shakes—energy drinks—on his Web site. Christian Fitness Shakes. He says they have given him such strength that he can leg-press 2,000 pounds.

The average leg-press machine has a maximum of 400 pounds. The professional ones, about 1,000 pounds. Pat claims he leg-presses 2,000.

To paraphrase the old Steven Wright punch line, "Not all at once."

Pat Robertson*, today's Worst Person in the World!*

She Stands

MAY 24, 2006

The bronze is shared by Larry and Ashley Gargis of Hillsboro, Alabama. Police say they had shoplifted a "king-sized marital aid" from a local, uh, boutique. Apparently they liked it, because three weeks later they went back to the same store, where the clerk recognized them.

The "king-sized marital aid" was recovered, but, according to police spokesman Chris Mathews—seriously, Chris Mathews—"basically, the store manager declined taking it back. Ha!" (OK, I'm embellishing here. *That* Chris Mathews didn't say "Ha!" in connection with this story. Only my MSNBC colleague Chris *Matthews* says "Ha!")

Runner-up: David McCann, who had spent the last two years as a phys ed teacher in the Orlando school system. Evidently he was very qualified. Police say two officers found him shouting at passersby that he was Luke Skywalker. When he wouldn't leave, they unsuccessfully tried to handcuff him.

A baton and a stun gun didn't stop him either. As the police report reads, Mr. McCann "continued to attack with super human strength." It took four officers to bring him down. With kryptonite.

But our winner . . .

Bill's version of an 18-year-old Kentucky girl getting $4,000 in tuition assistance for winning an ACLU essay contest? That Shannon Baldon was "getting a scholarship for refusing to stand for the Pledge of Allegiance—very nice." In fact, as Shannon's father, the Air Force vet, tells the *Louisville Courier-Journal*, "she stands" for the pledge.

Bill? Swing and a miss.

Bill O'Reilly, *today's Worst Person in the World!*

Mr. Wrong and Ms. Right

MAY 25, 2006

The bronze to John Gomes of Boston, currently on trial there for murder. Apparently he didn't think his lawyer was doing enough to convince the jury he was innocent, so he tried to strangle his lawyer in the courtroom.

"Uhh, the jury will disregard that attempted murder."

The runner-up: Stephen Brandt of New York. He apparently got his idea for a class-action lawsuit from a *Seinfeld* episode, but a judge has now thrown out his case against a low-fat ice cream maker. Brandt says the stuff was not low fat, and eating it actually caused him to gain weight.

But in a deposition he admitted he also "regularly ate traditional ice cream, McDonald's and Wendy's cheeseburgers, French fries, pepperoni pizza, beer, corn chips, doughnuts, cookies, hard cheese, eggs, bagels, peanut butter, Chinese take out food, and pasta," and he didn't exercise.

"Uhh, the jury will disregard that Bundt cake."

But the winner . . .

What a streak! This is like Cal Ripken. After unsuccessfully trying to kiss the butt of Natalie Mains and the Dixie Chicks, Billo's back on the warpath, ranting that the band is "far left" and "No far right person in this country is going to get the cover of *Time* magazine as the Dixie Chicks are this week. There's not a far right person in this country going to get on the cover of *Time* magazine. Not gonna happen."

Uh, Bill, what about when Ann Coulter was on the cover of *Time* Magazine?

Unless that was just some guy who looked like Ann Coulter.

Bill O'Reilly, *today's Worst Person in the World!*

What's One More Massacre?

MAY 31, 2006

Number three: Ad Van Den Berg, one of the founders of Holland's Charity, Freedom, and Diversity political party. Nice name. Except their only political aim is to lower the age of consent from 16 to 12.

They're pedophiles.

Conveniently, in a recent poll in Holland, 82 percent of respondents said the government should do something to outlaw the party, let alone pedophilia.

Number two: Vernon Robinson, a far-right Republican seeking the congressional seat from the 13th district of North Carolina. He's setting a lovely tone for this year's campaign by running a radio ad in which he says if his opponent "had his way, America would be nothing but one big fiesta for illegal aliens and homosexuals."

Gay-bashing, immigrant-bashing, Hispanic-bashing. You left out Terry Schiavo.

But our winner . . .

John Gibson, claiming the lead in the race for the biggest rationalization of Haditha: "If Iraqis know their own history, they know massacres have been committed in Iraq by warring parties for millennia piled on millennia. This is the part of the world that was in on the massacre game early . . ."

Well! That's all right, then! What's one more massacre?

John Gibson*, today's Worst Person in the World!*

The Worst in Show

JUNE 1, 2006

We wanted to end this on the same thread of jest that I've always hoped meandered through—on occasion extremely faintly—the nightly "Worst Person" segments. But the malice and pigheadedness that all the nominees seem to have has climaxed in one final eruption from the inspiration for all this. Jesting is invaluable, even soul-saving. But sometimes it must rest and let outrage take the stage. For dimwittedness is dimwittedness, and buffoonery is buffoonery. But facts are facts—and screwing with them for some cryptic rationalization of atrocity is unforgivable.

Abraham Lincoln did not shoot John Wilkes Booth. *Titanic* did not sink a north Atlantic iceberg. And Fox News is neither fair nor balanced. These are facts intelligible to all adults, most children, and some of your more discerning domesticated animals. But not to Bill-O.

The guilty pleasure offered by the existence of Bill O'Reilly is simple but understandable: 99 times out of 100, when we belly up to the Bill-O bar of bluster, we partake of the movable falafel feast—he serves us nothing but comedy, farce, slapstick, unconscious self-mutilation. The Sideshow Bob of commentators forever stepping on the same rake, forever muttering the same grunted, inarticulate surrender, forever resuming the circle that will take him back to the same rake. The Sisyphus of morons, if you will.

But this is the 100th time out of 100. It is not funny at all. Bill O'Reilly has, for the second time in under eight months, slandered at least 84 dead American servicemen. He has turned them again from victims of the kind of atrocity our country has always fought against into perpetrators of that kind of atrocity. He has made these Americans into war criminals. They are dead and have been dead for 61 years. They cannot defend themselves against O'Reilly. We will have to do it for them.

Last October Bill O'Reilly railed against a ruling that more photos from the infamous Abu Ghraib prison in Iraq might be released. His guest on his program was Wesley Clark. Clark is a retired four-star general, was for four years supreme Allied commander of NATO in Europe. First in his class at West Point, wounded in Vietnam, earned the Bronze star and the Silver Star, and has streets named for him in Alabama and in Kosovo. Therefore, naturally, O'Reilly knows much more about the military than General Clark does. Clark defended the release of the additional Abu Ghraib photos, saying we need to know what happened and to correct it. O'Reilly lectured him and concluded that there had always been atrocities, even by Americans in war.

"General," Bill declared, "you need to look at the Malmédy Massacre in World War II in the 82nd airborne."

It was a remarkable mistake. The Belgian town of Malmédy did lend its name to one of the most appalling battlefield war crimes of the twentieth century. But O'Reilly's implication that the Americans committed it was entirely backward. Americans, most of them members of the Battery B of the 285th Fuel Artillery Observation Battalion, surrendered to German Panzer troops and were then shot by the S.S. Yet O'Reilly had implied that the Americans had massacred these Germans in this one stark moment of the Battle of the Bulge. And he used this Alice-through-the-looking-glass view of history to somehow rationalize Abu Ghraib while trying to dress down a four-star American general.

Still, it could have been a mistake. We make them. Even historians do. O'Reilly had not explicitly called the Americans the war criminals of Malmédy. Our war troops, too, were accused of crimes against prisoners in the Second World War. It was assumed last year that he had simply made a foolish error, and though he got beaten up appropriately in some places, it was all largely dismissed as merely that, a mistake.

On Tuesday, May 30, O'Reilly's guest was again General Wes Clark. This time the topic was the apparent murder of Iraqi civilians at Haditha. That O'Reilly was dismissive of that event should be no surprise. That he should have described as the real crime of Iraq the events of Abu Ghraib should be no surprise to those who know of his willingness to jettison his most important beliefs of yesterday for the expediencies and the ratings of today. But that he should have brought up Malmédy again, that was a surprise.

"In Malmédy, as you know," Bill intoned, "U.S. forces captured SS forces who had their hands in the air and they were unarmed and they shot them down. You know that. That's on the record. And documented."

Thus was the full depth of Bill O'Reilly's insult to the American debt of World War II made clear. The mistake of last October was not some innocent slip or misremembered history. This was the way O'Reilly understood it, and, thus, this way it had to be. No errors corrected, no apologies offered, no stopping the relentless tide of bull even briefly enough to check one fact.

The facts of Malmédy are terrifying as described by Michael Reynolds in his painstakingly detailed article from a 2003 issue of *World War II* magazine. One week before Christmas, 1944, 139 U.S. soldiers, most of them from the 285th Field Artillery, encountered the German Kampfgruppe Peiper, the leading formation of the German 1st SS Panzer Division, one of only two German units in the entire war that actually carried Adolf Hitler's name. The Americans were overrun. Eleven of the 139 soldiers were killed in the very short battle of Malmédy, two more were killed as they tried to flee, seven escaped, six became prisoners of war. The other 113 Americans, nearly all of whom had surrendered outright, were ordered to assemble in an open field next to a restaurant, the Café Bodarwé.

What happened next has been attributed to many things: a cold-blooded decision by that Panzer unit's commander, SS Lt. Colonel Joachim Peiper, that he could not handle the prisoners; or an unjustifiable overreaction to some kind of escape attempt; or simply horrible mass murder.

Within 15 minutes Peiper or someone directly under him had ordered his men to shoot the unarmed American POWs. The bodies at Malmédy were not found until a month later. There were 84 of them, all American soldiers, more than half with gunshot wounds to their heads. Six had received fatal blows to the head. Nine were found with their arms still raised above their heads. The fact that O'Reilly got these horrible facts completely backward twice offended even his usually compliant viewers.

The next night O'Reilly read an email from Donn Caldwell of Fort Worth, Texas. "Bill," Caldwell wrote, "you mentioned Malmedy [sic] as the site of an American massacre during World War II. It was the other way around, the SS shot down U.S. prisoners."

Bill responded: "In the heat of the debate with General Clark, my statement wasn't clear enough, Mr. Caldwell. *After* Malmédy, some German captors were executed by American troops."

Wrong answer.

When you are that wrong, when you are defending Nazi war criminals and pinning their crimes on Americans and you get caught doing so twice, you're supposed to say, I'm sorry, I was wrong, and then you're supposed to shut up for a long time. Instead, Fox washed its transcript of O'Reilly's remarks Tuesday. Its Web site claims O'Reilly said "in Normandy," when, in fact, as freely available clips of the show prove, he said "in Malmédy.'"

The rewriting of past reporting worthy of George Orwell has now carried over into such online transcription services as Burell's and Factiva. Whatever did or did not happen later in supposed or actual retribution, the victims at Malmédy were Americans, gunned down while surrendering by Nazis in 1944 and again by a false patriot who would rather be loud than right.

Fortunately, after we called out O'Reilly and Fox on both his slander of dead American soldiers and their attempt to hide it, Fox changed the transcription back. It now reads as it should have all along. As O'Reilly said it, "In Malmédy, as you know."

The question is: Why has Bill O'Reilly twice turned the dead victims of Nazi war atrocities into American war criminals, and perhaps worse, offered no apology or clarification other than a tepid 24-word dismissal?

His blasé response to his own malicious remarks suggests he still has some doubts about the truthfulness of the story of Malmédy. Turns out others have preceded him down this road of anti-American doubt. A series of speeches, articles, and lawsuits in this country in 1949 suggested that evidence and confessions of those German soldiers who admitted what they had done at Malmédy had been obtained under torture, torture by American Jewish prosecutors and servicemen. Malmédy, the murder by the SS of 84 American soldiers who had just surrendered, had been transformed into some sort of Jewish propaganda plot, and an ad hoc investigation was launched by the Senate Armed Services Committee.

One of its members was an obscure junior senator from Wisconsin, Joseph McCarthy. But within five months of its formation, that senate subcommittee on which McCarthy served had found nothing to support the charges that Malmédy was a fiction. Its senior members, Republican Raymond Baldwin of Connecticut and Democrat Estes Kefauver of Tennessee, determined that the medical evidence was to the contrary and that the only thing supporting the charges was prejudice and a desire by some in the German American community to blunt the impact of the then ongoing Nazi war crimes tribunal.

That's when Senator Joseph McCarthy quit the committee and accused Senators Baldwin and Kefauver of "whitewashing the investigation." Senator Joe McCarthy and evidently Bill O'Reilly believe the real victims were the Nazis.

"In Malmédy, as you know," Bill O'Reilly said on the air Tuesday night in some indecipherable attempt to defend the events of Haditha, "U.S. forces captured SS forces who had their hands in the air and were unarmed and they shot them dead. You know that. That's on the record. And documented." The victims in Malmédy in December 1944 were Americans, Americans with their hands in the air, Americans who were unarmed. That's on the record and documented, and their memory deserves better than Bill O'Reilly.

We all do.